cooks'
books

cooks' books

A definitive collection of

50 CLASSIC RECIPES

for everyday life

Carolyn Hart

in association with

Telegraph magazine

First published in Great Britain by Simon & Schuster UK Ltd, 2005
A Viacom Company

Simon & Schuster UK Ltd
Africa House
64–78 Kingsway
London
WC2B 6AH

1 3 5 7 9 10 8 6 4 2

Design: Eye For Design
Illustrator: Brian Gough
Cover illustrator: Jonny Hannah
Copy editor: Nicole Foster
Proofreader: Nicole Foster
Indexer: Anne Doggett

A CIP catalogue record of this book is available from the British Library

ISBN 07432 7535 7

Printed in Great Britain

For
Sophie, Max and Clementine

Contents

*Women can spin very well; but they cannot make
a good book of cookery –*

Samuel Johnson

God made food, the devil made cooks –

James Joyce

Masticate, Denticate, Chump, Grind, and Swallow –

Dr Kitchiner

Acknowledgements

So many people have helped me in so many ways with
the compiling of this book – not least the chefs who
provided the recipes (and let me use them here. Thank
you). But I owe a special thanks to John Walsh who has
been an unfailing source of love and encouragement,
quotes, suggestions and even the odd rewrite; to my
children who uncomplainingly eat the results of my forays
into the kitchen; and to my parents who started it all.

I'd also like to thank Rose Prince whose help and
advice have been invaluable; Chris Hirst for ... well,
just being there; Geoff Nicholson who kept me supplied
with books and food; Louise Allen-Jones for her advice
about green chicken bones; Michele Lavery who
commissioned the original *Telegraph* column on which
this book is based; and, not least, the shades of
Elizabeth David, Alan Davidson and Jane Grigson
without whom there probably wouldn't be any
contemporary classic cooks' books.

Conversion tables

The recipes in this book come from a variety of sources and some date from before the metric era. The tables below give approximate conversions.

Weights		Volume	
½ oz	15 g	½ fl oz	15 ml
1 oz	25 g	1 fl oz	30 ml
2 oz	60 g	2 fl oz	50 ml
3 oz	75 g	5 fl oz (¼ pint)	150 ml
4 oz	110 g	10 fl oz (½ pint)	300 ml
5 oz	140 g	15 fl oz (¾ pint)	425 ml
6 oz	175 g	1 pint	600 ml
7 oz	200 g	1¾ pints	1 litre
8 oz	225 g		
9 oz	250 g		
10 oz	285 g		
12 oz	350 g		
1 lb	450 g		
1½ lb	700 g		
2 lb	900 g		
3 lb	1.35 kg		
5 lb	2.25 kg		

Lengths

⅛ inch	3 mm
¼ inch	5 mm
½ inch	1 cm
1 inch	2.5 cm
2 inches	5 cm
3 inches	7.5 cm
4 inches	10 cm
5 inches	13 cm
6 inches	15 cm
7 inches	18 cm
8 inches	20cm
9 inches	23 cm
10 inches	25 cm
12 inches	30 cm

Introduction

I have many cookbooks in my kitchen, collected over
the years; sometimes it seems there are hundreds
of the things, sometimes there are not nearly enough.
Some are quite old but (when you've retrieved them
from a top shelf or from behind the radiator) strangely
unused. Some are brand new and untried, yet to yield
up any exciting new culinary ideas. A few, though,
are regularly thumbed, some of their colour spreads
discoloured with wineglass rings and spattered with
basting fat, while the rest of the book remains pristine.

It occurred to me, one day, that however many cookery
books I possess, I probably use regularly only one or
two recipes at most from each, and I use those over
and over again. It further occurred to me, as I prepared
to make Yorkshire pudding, that although I knew the
recipe like an old friend, I'd no idea which book it came
from, or where that book might be. After searching
through several candidates, I found one in which the
pages containing the Yorkshire Pudding recipe were
stuck together. Wouldn't it be easier, I thought, if all
the recipes you used constantly (and that includes the

ones in newspaper cuttings and on the backs of foreign postcards) were contained in one book? A definitive collection of, say, 50 classic dishes that will get you through life as one generally, messily, lives it – which means recipes for dinner parties; hangover breakfasts; comfort food for ill children; speedy, post-work suppers and all the rest.

That was the germ of this book. When I started writing it, I realised that most of the recipes I use constantly are also the ones good enough to withstand the daily frustration of never having exactly the right ingredients, or enough of the right ingredients, for the thing you've decided to cook while sitting on the Tube home. Imaginative substitution is a long-standing feature of my cooking. I am not so unreasonable as a friend of mine who will dispatch her husband into the night at half past ten in search of star anise, just because the recipe says you need it. All the things I cook must either fit a completely different set of ingredients from the ones originally listed or be immune to substitutions.

They also have to be recipes which can be carried out while doing several other things at the same time – locating a wine bottle, finding a clean glass, answering questions about Stalin and electromagnetic fields, looking for lost items of clothing, doing mental arithmetic, composing first sentences for other people's novels and talking on the telephone. I don't think there's anything in this book which requires that you stand over it for longer than three minutes at a time and, apart from one recipe, nothing that needs absolutely accurate measurements.

Apicius, the notorious Roman cook whose collection of recipes is the only one to survive from the Roman era, was famously cavalier about measurements and ingredients. He once wrote a recipe for a sauce of immensely complicated structure which only in the last paragraph mentioned the main ingredient over which the sauce was to be poured – an enormous after thought: 'In a mortar put pepper, lovage, coriander-seed, mint, rue. Pound, moisten with liquamen, add honey and wine and blend with liquamen. Dry the hot boiled pig with a clean cloth and pour the dressing over.'

You can find exponents of the Apicius way throughout the history of cooking – and, I was pleased to see recently, in contemporary literature too. In Ian McEwan's novel *Saturday*, 'What he likes about cooking', Perowne, the hero, muses as he prepares to embark on a fish stew, 'is its relative imprecision and lack of discipline... The cookery writers he admires speak of "handfuls" and "a sprinkling", of "chucking in" this or that. They list alternative ingredients and encourage experimentation.' You could make Perowne's rather delicious-sounding fish stew simply by reading the rest of this paragraph (p. 177, if you're interested), never mind that McEwan doesn't include a single measurement or cooking time. That's my kind of cooking.

Reading, it seems to me, is inextricably linked with cooking. All the best cookbooks, and indeed the best cookery writers, give you quantities of extraneous detail about the food they're encouraging you to cook. Often you get to hear about their domestic lives too, which adds to the attraction – sometimes one feels like just reading the book and sending out for a takeaway instead. All the recipes in this book come with a history. They have descended down the generations, through the hands of people like Robert May, Queen Elizabeth I's chef, the rather scary Hugh Plat whose recipe for hair dye would almost certainly have killed you, Hannah Glasse, Mrs Beeton, Elizabeth David and Jane Grigson, right down to our own notable practitioners of the culinary arts – Fergus Henderson, Prue Leith, Simon Hopkinson, Rose Prince, Mark Hix and Nigel Slater. I like to know that the recipe for Georgian Pheasant donated by some unknown Russian family to the *Cookbook of the*

United Nations in 1964, a favourite in my house, was
also used by Jane Grigson, who got it from Escoffier,
who borrowed it from *La Gastronomie en Russie* by
A. Petit (1860). Equally, Nigel Slater's 'Monday night
supper' of leftover roast beef fried up with cabbage and
a dash of red wine, goes straight back to Dr Kitchiner's
recipe for Bubble and Squeak in his *Cook's Oracle*
published in 1817. I like the idea that we are all
connected to the generations of families that have gone
before us, through the food we cook for our own families
today – with a bit of luck this book, with its collection
of classic recipes culled from many contemporary
and historical sources, will help to carry on that tradition.

Meat

Beef

'The English men understand almost better than any other people the art of properly roasting a joint, which is also not to be wondered at; because the art of cooking as practised by most English men does not extend much beyond roast beef and plum pudding' – Per Kalm, 1748

Roast beef

'One man's meat', as Mel Calman once famously wrote, or in his case drew, 'is another woman's Sunday gone.' Well, how true ... but I love cooking Sunday lunch – provided I'm doing it for a lot of people. It takes pretty much the same amount of time and effort to do it for three as it does for ten, so why skimp on the guests? If it's roast beef you're after, go for a three- or four-bone rib, as big as you can fit in the oven. Preheat the oven to 220°C/425°F/gas mark 7. Weigh the joint and calculate the cooking time – the rarer the better: 14 minutes per 500 g (or 13 minutes per lb) plus

15 minutes for rare meat, 18 minutes per 500 g
(or 16 minutes per lb) plus 20 minutes for medium.
Do not even consider roasting it for longer.

Put the joint in a roasting tin, fat side up and smear
the fat with mustard. Season with salt and pepper.
You should put the Yorkshire puddings in (if you are
doing them as individuals) about 15 minutes before
the end of cooking, so that they can finish off while
the beef rests outside the oven (and make that about
half an hour before the end of cooking if you're doing
them in one pan).

Yorkshire pudding

As every Yorkshire inhabitant will tell you, Yorkshire
puddings can only really be made successfully by
people who live in Yorkshire. Their southern counterparts
– the puddings, not the people – are softer and heavier.
The crispness of true Yorkshire pudding comes from
putting the batter into a pan in which the oil is smoking
hot. Yorkshire puddings weren't eaten exclusively with
beef, either – one of the first recipes for a batter pudding was published in *The Whole Duty of a Woman* in
1737. It used a pancake batter fried in a little butter
in a pan and put under a shoulder of mutton, 'keeping
frequently shaking it by the handle and it will be light

and savoury, and fit to take up when your mutton is
enough'. Ten years later, Hannah Glasse gave a similar
recipe, calling it 'a yorkshire pudding' (her recipe went:
a quart of milk, 4 eggs and a little salt, made into
a thick batter with flour).

Yorkshire pudding traditionally comes in one piece. You
can of course make individual puddings but 'this is not
the authentic Yorkshire method,' says Alan Davidson,
editor of the magisterial *Penguin Companion to Food*.
'Strictly speaking, the pudding, cut into squares, should
be served with gravy before the meat, to take the edge
off the appetite.'

The best Yorkshire pudding is my mother's. Like
Hannah Glasse, she comes from the north. She cooks
it in one whole piece with roast beef, but also serves
up individual Yorkshire puddings as a dessert, with
melted butter and brown sugar. Since I've never seen
my mother's recipe actually written down, I've always
used the version in Jane Grigson's *English Food*.
Grigson, incidentally, remembered her grandfather
keeping the Yorkshire pudding on the table after the
roast beef had gone back to the kitchen, to be
'finished up with sweetened condensed milk',
a practice which upset his wife, who prided herself
on her fancy puddings.

Yorkshire pudding

(from *English Food* by Jane Grigson)

Serves 4–6

> ¼ lb flour
> a pinch of salt
> 1 egg
> ½ pint milk, or ¼ pint each milk and water

Mix the flour and salt into a bowl and make a well in
the centre. Break in the egg and add a little milk.
Beginning at the centre, stir these ingredients into
a batter, gradually pouring in the remainder of the milk,
or milk and water. Pour a little oil into a high-sided
baking tin, or into each section of an individual tart tin
and heat in the oven (about 180–200°C/350–400°F/gas
mark 4–6). When the oil is hot, pour in the batter and
put in the hot oven. Bake for about 35–40 minutes
if in one piece, about 15–20 minutes if in individual
puddings, or until brown and crisp on top. Serve
immediately with the roast.

Roast potatoes

For the roast potatoes, I'd turn straight to Nigel Slater –
'Crisp, gooey, sticky, melting, golden and crusty...' he
enthuses seductively, 'but the best one of all is the one
stuck to the side of the roasting tin, the seriously fatty,
crusty, gungy one.' In *Real Cooking* Slater devotes four
whole pages to roast potatoes, including spiced roast
potatoes, potatoes roasted with whole garlic cloves,
and roast balsamic potatoes. This is his unbeatable
recipe for the plain ordinary kind. You can also dust
them lightly with flour pre-roasting, which gives them
a really crispy skin, or even roll them in couscous,
which will make them particularly crunchy.

Roast potatoes

(from *Real Cooking* by Nigel Slater)

Serves 4

> *900 g/about 5 large floury potatoes,*
> *such as King Edwards*
> *salt*
> *lard, dripping, goose fat or fat from the roast*

Peel the potatoes and cut them into suitably sized chunks. Put them into a saucepan of cold water and bring to the boil. Add salt and turn down to a simmer. Give them a good 5 minutes at a rolling boil, until they are slightly soft round the edges. Drain the water off and return the pan to the heat. Shake the pan so that the edge of the potatoes are scuffed. This will give them wonderfully crunchy frilly edges. Tip the potatoes into a shallow metal pan in which you have heated the fat then bake in a preheated oven at 200°C/400°F/gas mark 6 until golden and crisp – 45 minutes, maybe even longer. The best roast spuds are those cooked in the pan with the roasting meat.

Tagliata di manzo

My friend Louise's recipe for tagliata is one of the wonders of modern cookery – it's delicious every time and constantly asked for by my children, who gallingly consider it a great deal better than anything I can come up with. It is the quintessential summer dish, cold rare roast beef laid out on a plate with a scattering of fresh tarragon and shelled baby broad beans and drizzled with extra virgin oil and balsamic vinegar. Unfortunately, Louise's tagliata is also a carefully guarded secret –

'No, I am not telling you, or anyone, how I make it...' – so this is a mongrel version culled from a variety of sources.

Consolingly, Anna del Conte, in her *Concise Gastronomy of Italy*, calls tagliata 'a modern dish launched in restaurants and now quite popular', which puts it in its place. Her version consists of a T-bone steak (about 5 cm/2 inches thick) cooked until still red inside and then sliced across diagonally to a thickness of 2 cm (³/₄ inch). It is served with best olive oil and plenty of pepper.

tagliata

Serves 3–4

> *3–4 lean fillet steaks about 2.5 cm (1 inch) thick*
> *rocket leaves or lamb's lettuce*
> *extra virgin olive oil*
> *a bunch of tarragon*
> *salt and pepper*

Season the steaks with salt and pepper and fry in a smoking hot pan for 1 minute each side for very rare;

$1\frac{1}{2}$ minutes each side for rare. Slice the steaks thinly diagonally across. Place the rocket or lamb's lettuce leaves on a large platter, and lay the sliced steaks slightly overlapping on top. Drizzle with plenty of olive oil and scatter over the tarragon leaves. Season with sea salt and freshly ground black pepper. It makes a wonderful al fresco Sunday lunch main course.

Beef casserole Niçoise

This was the first dinner party dish I ever cooked, possibly the *only* thing I ever cooked for years. It came from *The Pauper's Cookbook* by Jocasta Innes. Ms Innes's approach is refreshingly down to earth. Her book is divided into sections labelled: 'Padding', 'Dieting on the cheap', 'Standards' and 'Fancy work'. 'Improvisation is the key word here,' she asserts at one point, and her list of necessary kitchen implements is startlingly short: egg-whisk, wooden spoons, metal spatula, coffee strainer, a grater, a knife and two saucepans.

The beef casserole came from the Standards section, and it always looked spectacular and smelt wonderful, gorgeously red and aromatic, and the olives made it seem (back in the 80s) amazingly sophisticated. It was almost invariably followed by ginger-biscuit pudding – the other thing I knew how to make (a packet of ginger biscuits, each dipped in sherry and sandwiched together in a roll with whipped cream. You covered the roll with the remainder of the cream and it was utterly delicious). In retrospect, I don't remember ever putting the dash of vinegar into the stew, preferring to use red wine instead. Now, I'd cook it with a bottle of red, bunging that in at the same time as the tomatoes.

Beef casserole Niçoise

(from *The Pauper's Cookbook* by Jocasta Innes)

Serves 4–6

> *1 kg (2 lb) shin of beef*
> *125 g (4 oz) bacon*
> *3 onions, coarsely chopped*
> *3 carrots, thinly sliced*
> *olive oil*
> *3 cloves of garlic, peeled and chopped*
> *10–12 stoned black olives*
> *1 medium tin peeled tomatoes*
> *wine vinegar*

1–2 bay leaves
small bunches of parsley, thyme
  and rosemary, chopped
salt and pepper

Preheat the oven to 180°C/350°F/gas mark 4. Cut the
beef into thick pieces and the bacon into small strips.
Heat some oil in a heatproof, ovenproof casserole.
Put the bacon strips in and then the meat and onions.
Turn the meat slices until brown all over. Add the tinned
tomatoes and a dash of wine vinegar and the garlic,
carrots, herbs, salt and pepper. Heat together on a
medium heat until the stew simmers. Remove from the
heat, cover and transfer to the oven and cook for
2½ hours. At the end of this time, add the olives and
cook, covered, for half an hour longer. If necessary add
boiling water thickened with tomato purée, but the
sauce should be thick. Serve with rice or baked potatoes.

Mutton and lamb

'Bold and erect the Caledonian stood/Old was his mutton
and his claret was good' – John Home, 1822
'Vicarage mutton: hot on Sunday, cold on Monday, hashed
on Tuesday, minced on Wednesday, curried on Thursday,
broth on Friday, cottage pie Saturday' – Dorothy Hartley,

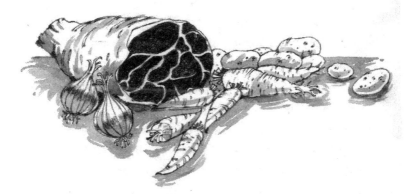

Although mutton was once a mainstay of British cuisine –
it was used as a pie filling from the 17th century
onwards (Dr Johnson was very fond of Scottish mutton
pie), was eaten with oysters, anchovies, lemon slices
and redcurrant jelly during the 18th century, and was
a favourite of Mrs Beeton in the 19th – it pretty much
disappeared in the 20th century. Most of the recipes
used for mutton are now applied to lamb, from Irish stews
and hotpot to roasts. But mutton is beginning to enjoy
a revival, partly due to the recent championship by Prince
Charles, who launched 'Mutton Renaissance' in 2004,
saying, 'When I was growing up mutton was one of my
favourite dishes, but it has all but disappeared over
the last 30 or 40 years.' Prince Charles launched his
campaign at the Ritz in London where mutton, under
the auspices of John Williams the head chef, is firmly

on the menu. You can buy an excellent Cumbrian air-dried mutton at Borough Market in London from Andrew Sharp (www.farmersharp.co.uk or info@farmersharp.co.uk).

In her book of recipes published after the war, Alice B. Toklas recounts the extravagant preparation of a leg of mutton given to her friend Madame Pierlot by 'a surgeon living in the French provinces'. It was radically different from anything that might have been served up in England. It began: eight days in advance 'cover the leg of mutton with a marinade of old Burgundy, Beaune or Chambertin and virgin olive oil. Into this balm to which you have already added salt, pepper, bay leaf, thyme, an atom of ginger root, put a pinch of cayenne, a nutmeg cut into small pieces, a handful of crushed juniper berries and a dessertspoon of powdered sugar. Twice a day you will turn the gigot. After you have placed the gigot in the marinade arm yourself with a surgical syringe of a size to hold half a pint which you will fill with half a cup of cognac and half a cup of fresh orange juice. Inject the contents of the syringe into the gigot in three different spots. Each day you will fill the syringe with the marinade and inject the contents into the gigot. At the end of the week, the leg of mutton is ready to be roasted.' Years later and much to her surprise, since she had assumed that the syringe was a piece of French whimsy, Toklas found the

recipe in Bertrand Guegan's *Le Grand Cuisinier Français.*
It might be easier to make a stew. Henry Moore, the
sculptor, had a recipe for lamb stew which appeared in
The Artist's Cookbook, decorated, in a seamless blend
of art and ingredients, with Moore's sheep. His stew
was a classic combination of lamb chops, potatoes,
onions and mushrooms, wine, stock, breadcrumbs and
cream, seasoned with a bay leaf and sprinkled with
chopped parsley. It's the sophisticated version of Irish
stew which, at least in *The Ballymaloe Cookbook* by
Myrtle Allen, adds mutton fat and carrots and uses
water instead of wine, but even this is sophistication
itself compared to the lamb stew described by Marthe
Pampille Daudet in her book *Pampille's Table* (1919).
Proust makes several references to Pampille, wife of
the poet Alphonse Daudet's son Leon, in *À La Recherche
du Temps Perdu,* usually through the persona of a
nostalgic Mme de Guermantes, but once with reference
to M. Verdurin who 'died at the right moment, *à point,*
as the lobsters, grilled according to Pampille's
incomparable recipe, are going to be.'

Pampille's Table was an attempt to 'group together some
of the best traditional recipes of French cooking and to
present the most characteristic recipes from each
region', but although it revels in the culinary delights of

Burgundy and Brittany, Provence and Savoy, when it comes to the Auvergne, its tone changes drastically: the Auvergnat is 'stingy', Pampille writes sternly, and has no ambition beyond a bowl of Soupe aux Choux. For more festive occasions, he will cook up leg of lamb with potatoes, though he is quite likely to do this 'without the leg of lamb'.

Lamb goulash

The lamb recipe that really repays the effort comes from a *Good Housekeeping* magazine, circa 1995. It's better cooked for 2 hours (especially if you double the quantities) and don't use smoked paprika – it's too powerful a flavour. Always use a fresh tub of paprika, as it doesn't keep well.

Paprika lamb goulash

(from *Good Housekeeping*)

Serves 4

> *1 Spanish onion*
> *900 g neck of lamb, trimmed of fat*

50 g unsalted butter
1 heaped teaspoon flour
3 teaspoons sweet paprika
sea salt, pepper
150 ml red wine
1 small tin chopped tomatoes
To serve:
125 ml crème fraîche
flat leaf parsley, chopped

Preheat oven to 220°C/425°F/gas mark 7. Peel, halve and slice onion thinly, then cut meat into decent-sized chunks. Heat butter in frying pan over low heat and sweat the onion until it's translucent and soft, then place onion in casserole. Turn up the heat under the pan, add meat in batches and cook until it changes colour to brown, then add flour, paprika and seasoning, and stir around for a moment. Transfer meat to the casserole, pour over the wine and add the tomatoes. Cover and cook in the oven for at least 1½ hours until meat is tender and surrounded by rich juices. Serve with a spoonful of crème fraîche and chopped parsley.

Shepherd's pie

Shepherd's pie used to be made on Mondays from the leftover meat on the joint, which your mother put through a mincer that was clipped on to the edge of the kitchen table. If it was leftover lamb, it was shepherd's pie; leftover beef made cottage pie. Now, when mincers have pretty much disappeared from modern kitchens – sometimes you can find them at car boot sales or in stylish retro kitchen shops – and you can buy two-for-one packs of mince in supermarkets, you can make shepherd's pie any day of the week.

I grew up with this dish and it has been so much part of my culinary life, that I don't think I have ever followed

a recipe for it. I've never met anyone who makes
shepherd's pie from a recipe that is identical to anyone
else's. Like Lego houses, they are structurally the
same but entirely different in essence. Mine used to
contain tomatoes and possibly even peas, but doesn't
any longer. In my opinion, it is absolutely the best
shepherd's pie you'll find, but you may think, 'How
can she put carrots in it?' or 'Flour? Is she mad?'

Well, sticking my neck out, I say you should boil 4 or 5
large potatoes (you don't even have to peel them as the
skin bakes into nice crispy bits later in the oven) and
while you're doing that, chop up an onion or two, 2 or 3
cloves of garlic and fry them lightly in a little olive oil.
Add about 500 g (1 lb 2 oz) lamb mince and fry for
about 10–15 minutes. Chop up 3–4 carrots while this is
happening and mash the potatoes (if they are ready) with
butter and milk. Now stir a tiny amount of flour (just a
dusting) into the frying mince and add a really hefty slug
of Worcestershire sauce. Stir all this around until it's
beginning to brown excitingly and then add stock, about
300 ml (½ pint) – you can use water instead if it's all
you've got – the chopped carrots and quite a lot of
chopped parsley. Add salt and pepper, and put the lot
into a fairly deep ovenproof dish. Cover with the mashed
potato and put in the oven (about 180°C/350°F/gas

mark 4) for at least 45 minutes until the potato has browned and the sauce is bubbling up over the sides.

Eat it immediately but leave a small amount for a solitary supper the next day – reheated shepherd's pie, baked to a crisp in the oven, is absolutely delicious. Hugh Fearnley-Whittingstall's recipe from *The River Cottage Meat Book* is a rather more sophisticated version of the above, using wine and leftover meat. I would leave out the ketchup altogether and use a lot more Worcestershire sauce.

Shepherd's pie

(from *The River Cottage Meat Book* by Hugh Fearnley-Whittingstall)

Serves 4–6

> *500 g leftover roast lamb*
> *1 tablespoon olive oil*
> *1–2 onions, chopped*
> *1–2 carrots, finely diced*
> *1 garlic clove, chopped*
> *any juices or gravy saved from*
> *   the joint or lamb stock*
> *½ glass red wine*

1 tablespoon tomato ketchup
1–2 teaspoons Worcestershire sauce
up to 1 kg creamy mashed potatoes
salt and pepper

Chop the meat into pea-sized pieces. Heat the oil in
a large frying pan or wide saucepan. Sweat the onions,
carrot and garlic in the oil until the carrots have softened
slightly. Add the meat and fry gently until brown. Add the
gravy, stock, wine, ketchup and Worcestershire sauce.
Season with salt and pepper. Simmer gently for a few
minutes, adding water if necessary. Add seasoning to
taste. Simmer gently for another 20–30 minutes, adding
liquid if necessary. The mixture should be well lubricated,
but not soupy. Put the meat in a pie dish and pile the
mashed potato on top, covering the meat completely.
Bake in a hot oven 200°C/400°F/gas mark 6 for 25–45
minutes until the mash is browned on top and the sauce
is bubbling up around the edges. Serve immediately.

Kidneys

'Mr Leopold Bloom ate with relish the inner organs
of beasts and fowls. He liked thick giblet soup, nutty
gizzards, a stuffed roast heart, liver slices fried with

*crustcrumbs, fried hencod's roes. Most of all he
liked grilled mutton kidneys which gave to his palate
a fine tang of faintly scented urine'* – James Joyce,
Ulysses, 1922

Before BSE, scrapie, scurvy, foot and mouth disease,
and all the myriad other ailments that afflict our national
livestock, the British used to cook kidneys on a regular
basis. There is an exotic recipe for them in *My Favourite
Recipes for Dainty Dishes* (1896, the author remains
anonymous), involving kidneys stuffed with oysters
and puréed mushrooms and served on warmed
half-tomatoes. Keith Floyd, in a 1989 pamphlet
unfortunately sponsored by Andrex, flamed them
dramatically in cognac, but a more usual way was to
cook them with sherry or mustard sauces, and dish
them up with rice.

Since they were also cheap, I can remember cooking
them often in my university days. Now my children would
rather eat bees than entertain the idea of consuming a
kidney, so secrecy and subterfuge is the order of the
day. So long as they don't know what it is they're eating,
they rather like them. The rise and rise of the tapas bar
has helped. A little dish of kidneys in sherry sauce with
bread and a glass of Spanish white in the Brindisa Bar

in Borough Market is as about as restorative as it gets.
Hugh Fearnley-Whittingstall's recipe for devilled kidneys
is the one to go for.

Devilled Kidneys

(from *The River Cottage Meat Book*
by Hugh Fearnley-Whittingstall)

Serves 2

> *4 lamb's kidneys, cut into quarters with the*
> *whitish core trimmed out*
> *a small glass of sherry*
> *1 tablespoon white wine or cider vinegar*
> *1 teaspoon redcurrant jelly*
> *a few good shakes of Worcestershire sauce*
> *a good pinch of cayenne pepper*
> *1 tablespoon English mustard*
> *1 tablespoon double cream*
> *a little chopped parsley*

Heat a little oil in a small frying pan, add the kidneys
and sizzle to brown them for just a minute, tossing them
occasionally in the pan. Then add a generous slosh of
sherry, let it bubble for a moment and follow up with a

more modest splash of wine or cider vinegar.

Add the redcurrant jelly and start to dissolve. Add the Worcestershire sauce, cayenne, mustard and plenty of black pepper. Season with a pinch of salt and take the edge off the fire with a spoonful of double cream. Bubble for another minute or two, shaking the pan occasionally until the sauce is reduced and nice and glossy. Season. Sprinkle with the parsley and serve with fried bread or boiled rice and a green salad.

Pork

'A sucking pig requires very careful roasting and like a young child must not be left for an instant' – Dr Kitchiner, 1804

'Any part of piggy/Is quite all right with me/Ham from Westphalia, ham from Parma/Ham as lean as the Dalai Lama' – Noel Coward, 1967

'A couple of flitches of bacon are worth fifty thousand Methodist sermons and religious tracts. They are great softeners of temper and promoters of domestic harmony' – William Cobbett, *Cottage Economy*, 1821

Gammon

Boiled gammon with cabbage is something that my other
half, the writer John Walsh, remembers from his Irish
childhood, and has assiduously encouraged his children
to eat. Luckily they love it and it's incredibly easy to do.
Boil a lump of smoked gammon in water for an hour or
so, skimming the fat off the top. Tear the leaves off the
cabbage stalks and rip them apart, remove the gammon
from the water and add the cabbage and cook in the
bacon water until tender. Serve the cabbage on a plate
with the gammon cut in great ignorant lumps on top.
Don't add any salt to the cabbage. If a more sophisticated
ham is called for, bake the gammon in the oven with
a glaze before serving. If you are starting from scratch,
you need to skin the ham and soak it overnight.

A ham and fags, as Alice B. Toklas's father, who had
managed to acquire two of them and 400 cigarettes
during the fire that broke out after the 1906 earthquake
in San Francisco, noted, allows you 'not only to exist
but be able to be hospitable'. In 1940, as the Germans
were advancing through France, and remembering her
father's advice, Toklas and Gertrude Stein did the
same. 'At Belley we bought two hams and hundreds
of cigarettes. The main road was filled with refugees...

... the firing grew louder. We lived on those two hams during the long lean winter that followed and well into the following spring, and the Eau de Vie de Marc in which they were cooked toned up winter vegetables. We threw nothing, but absolutely nothing, away.' Although it contains no eau-de-vie, there is a good recipe for baked ham in Henrietta Green's *Farmers' Market Cookbook;* it can also be found on the website www.foodloversbritain.com.

Baked ham

(from *Farmers' Market Cookbook* by Henrietta Green)

Serves 6–8

> *1.8 -kg (4 -lb) piece of gammon or ham*
> *1 whole onion*
> *5 cloves*
> *2 carrots, cut into chunks*
> *a handful of parsley stalks*
> *1 bay leaf*
> *5–6 black peppercorns*

For the glaze:

> *1 teaspoon dry mustard*
> *2 tablespoons black treacle*
> *2 tablespoons runny honey*
> *grated rind and juice of 1 orange*

Soak the ham overnight if necessary. To cook it, put it in a suitable saucepan and fill with water so the ham is submerged. Stud the onion with the cloves and put in the saucepan with the carrots, parsley, bay leaf and peppercorns. Bring to the boil and simmer for 1 hour 20 minutes (20 minutes per 500 g/1 lb 2 oz). Once cooked, lift the ham out and leave to cool. With a sharp knife, remove the skin and trim the fat to an even layer and score it into a diamond pattern (this makes the glaze stick to the surface more efficiently).

Preheat the oven to 190°C/375°F/gas mark 5. Mix all the ingredients for the glaze together and spread over the fat on the ham. Place in a baking tin in the oven and bake for about 20 minutes. If the glaze looks as though it's burning, cover with foil.

Sausages

To Make a Polonian Sawsedge, *'Take the fillets of a hog, chop them very small with a handful of red sage, season it hot with ginger and pepper and then put it into a great sheepes gut. Then let it lie three nights in brine; then boile it and hang it up a chimney where fire is usually kept, and these sawsedges will last one whole year'* – Sir Hugh Plat, *Delightes for Ladies...*, 1600

Although you may not be making your own sausages, and certainly not the Hugh Plat way (*Delightes for Ladies* also features a recipe entitled 'How to Colour the Head of Haire into a Chesnut Colour in Halfe an Houre' using 'oyle of vitriolle', lead, sulphur and quicklime: 'the longer it lyeth upon the haire the browner it groweth' – and the deader you'd be, presumably), cooking someone else's sausages is an underrated delight. I often think it a shame that sausages are relegated to nursery status, as they are so delicious (Robinsons the butchers in Stockbridge, Hants, is the place to buy them incidentally – they are the best in Britain, tel: 01264 810609).

In *Cooking in Ten Minutes* (1948), Edouard de Pomiane, Professeur at the Institut Pasteur in Paris, includes a strictly grown-up recipe for the classic combination of oysters and sausages, after which he recommends a salad, though not before, because 'it is too cheap. One eats too much because one is hungry at the beginning of a meal – and repents it five minutes later.' For two: 'Fry some chipolata sausages. Serve them very hot on a dish and on a second dish a dozen oysters. Alternate the sensations. Burn your mouth with a crackling sausage. Sooth your burns with a cool oyster. Continue until all the sausages and oysters have disappeared. White wine, of course.'

Elizabeth David combines red cabbage and frankfurters,
which makes a perfect late lunch on winter days. It
takes three to four hours, so stick it in the oven while
you go for a long walk. At the other end of the scale,
Jocasta Innes makes a Toad in the Hole which, she
notes scathingly, 'is not a dish for sophisticates but
an excellent way of stretching half a pound of chipolatas
into a solid meal for four people'. Use the Yorkshire
Pudding batter recipe, pre-fry some sausages, pour
the batter into a baking tin and drop in the sausages.
Bake in a brisk oven for 35 minutes or so.

Hugh Fearnley-Whittingstall has a much posher recipe in
The River Cottage Meat Book, which uses sausages and
pheasant breasts, slit and stuffed with prunes wrapped
in bacon, both encased in the batter, and which echoes
Mrs Beeton's Toad: 1½ pounds rump steak, I sheep's
kidney cooked in batter. 'Time: one and a half hours;
Average cost: 1s 9d; sufficient 4 or 5 persons'.

I'd go for the Elizabeth David recipe; the combination of
smoked sausage, red cabbage, spices and apples being
pretty much irresistible. I'd probably put in less wine
vinegar than she mentions, dispense with the peppers
and be more profligate with the orange peel.

Chou rouge landais

(from *French Country Cooking* by Elizabeth David)

> 1 medium-sized red cabbage,
>   sliced into thin strips
> 450 g (1 lb) cooking apples, peeled,
>   cored and sliced
> 450 g (1 lb) onions, sliced
> 2 smoked frankfurter sausages per person
> 150 ml (¼ pint) red wine
> 150 ml (¼ pint) wine vinegar
> 4 tablespoons brown sugar
> 2 sweet red peppers, cut into strips
> garlic
> a piece of dried orange peel
> herbs and seasoning, including mace,
>   ground cloves

In the bottom of a deep casserole put a layer of cabbage, then one of onions and then apples. Season with salt and pepper and add the herbs, mace and cloves, the garlic, the strips of pepper and the orange peel. Continue these layers until the casserole is full up. Moisten with the wine and vinegar. Cover and cook in in a very slow oven for 3–4 hours. Twenty minutes before serving add the sausages, buried deep in the

cabbage. Elizabeth David adds: 'To make the dish more
substantial, a few thick slices of bacon can be added.
A bacon or ham bone, or even bones from roast mutton
cooked with the cabbage and removed before serving,
enrich the flavour.'

Anna Haycraft and Caroline Blackwood have a similar
recipe in their inimitable book *Darling, You Shouldn't
Have Gone to So Much Trouble,* but use a small leg of
pork in place of the frankfurters. The dish is timed to
coincide with a walk to a pub, a drink, and a return walk.
'Chop cabbage and apple and put in a heavy casserole.
Add vinegar, garlic, sugar, salt and butter, and cover.
Rub the pork with oil and salt and wash the potatoes.
At 10.30 or 11 – depending on the size of the leg – put
the pork in a preheated oven (220°C/425°F/gas mark 7)
on the top shelf. At 11.30 or 45 – depending on the
distance of the pub from the oven – turn the heat down

to 200°C/400°F/gas mark 6. Put the closely covered cabbage on the middle shelf. Put the potatoes with butter and a little salt in another casserole, cover that closely and put it on the bottom oven shelf. When you return shortly after 2 pm, everything should be ready.'

You could conceivably combine this recipe with the one for Chou Rouge aux Marrons to be found in *Cooking With Nuts* by Oswell Blakeston. It's a surprisingly straightforward recipe for this eccentric book. Blakeston, a sensationalist Young British Artist long before Hirst and Emin came along, held art exhibitions in butcher's shops, produced short abstract films of the kind that now win the Turner Prize, and hung out in Fitzrovia, where he acquired the dubious accolade of being the only man to sleep with Dylan Thomas. Apart from cabbage with chestnuts, Blakeston included a recipe for the aquatic water caltrop ('a practical novelty for those who live near quiet ponds'), and one devised by the philosopher Dr Joad, designed to 'keep up epicurean standards in the lean days of rationing after the war' – tinned cuttlefish marinated in red wine and fried with oil, onions and a handful of nuts.

Marcel Boulestin served this Chou Rouge aux Marrons with goose, turkey, duck or chicken. Fry sliced red cabbage in butter, heat up the contents of a tin of chestnut purée, stir in 2 tablespoons of stock and season. Fry some bacon, mix it with the purée and pour the lot over the cabbage. I've tried this and though it tastes wonderful, it looks absolutely disgusting.

Rabbit

The astonishing revelation that Wild West novelist Zane Grey was once a dentist is compounded by the fact that he was also an excellent cook, albeit it chiefly an outdoor one. His son Romer described him as a 'meat-and-potatoes man' who also liked apple dumplings, but the *Zane Grey Cookbook* is really all about game, killing it as well as cooking it. It features such exotica as bear stew (although 'bears were incidental to my hunting trips'), elk heart pie and 'ruminant stroganoff', squirrel stew, and quick quail (not all that quick, presumably). His nearest English equivalent was probably Francis Trevelyan Buckland, a 19th-century eccentric who attempted to introduce eland to English dinner tables. As a child, Buckland had eaten dog, crocodile, roast giraffe and garden snails. He tried earwigs but thought them 'horribly bitter'. Until he ate a bluebottle, he considered mole to be the worst thing he had ever consumed.

Moles and bluebottles would presumably have been too small for Zane to bother about, but his book contains several recipes for rabbit. Rabbits, according to Zane, are North America's favourite game animal and he has several recipes for them, including Brunswick Stew, supposed to have been brought to Williamsburg by 'early Legislators'. Most of the Williamsburg recipes probably came straight from the kitchens of contemporary English country houses, many of which kept a home coney warren and used these wild-ish rabbits for pies and stews. In *Elinore Fettiplace's Receipt Book,* written in 1604 and edited by Hilary Spurling in 1986, there is a recipe for baked rabbit pie ('first cousin to Kenelm Digby's Excellent Hare-Pye'), which shows how baked pies were

used in Elizabethan times to preserve food. 'Before
the invention of canning, freezers or vacuum packs,'
Spurling explains, 'pies were convenient and relatively
durable portable food. Country people sent them by
coach across country as presents to friends in town,
or even over the Channel.' Nowadays, Spurling notes
sadly, if you don't possess a coney warren and 'have
to make do with frozen, imported or hutch rabbit, add
extra seasonings'.

Rabbit pie is one of those things you more often read
about than make – especially the raised pie kind, the
ones which were trundling across country in the 17th
century – and you're more likely to find your rabbit in
a casserole or stewed in mustard, like the classic dish
served up by Henry Harris at Racine. The following is
not the Racine version, but one which I inherited from
my grandmother and have adapted.

Rabbit with mustard

Serves 4

4–6 rabbit joints
15 g (1/2 oz) butter
olive oil
2 garlic cloves
1 small onion
150 ml (5 fl oz) of brandy or white wine
3–4 tablespoons grainy mustard
4–6 tablespoons cream or crème fraîche
chicken stock
chopped herbs – parsley, sage or tarragon

Season the rabbit joints with a dusting of flour, salt and pepper. Heat the butter and oil in a large heatproof pan and lightly brown the rabbit joints. Remove and set aside. Reduce the heat and fry the garlic and onion and cook for 5 minutes or so. Add the wine, mustard and cream and a little stock or water if necessary and let it bubble. Return the rabbit to the pan, cover and cook on a low heat until the rabbit is tender. Just before serving add the herbs, season and serve with boiled rice and green beans.

Chicken and game

'A person purchasing a fowl should not judge of its weight by appearance, as various arts are practised to impart a plump appearance which they do not possess. Above all, dealing with itinerant vendors should be carefully avoided; in most cases men clad in smock frocks and otherwise "got up" to represent the country dealers, are in reality artful denizens of London, who purchase the refuse stock at the large markets at nominal prices, and thus palm them off to the public at enormous profits' – The Dictionary of Daily Wants, 1859

Plus ça change and all that. When Henri IV of France generously indicated that he wished every peasant to have a chicken in his pot on Sundays, he could never have envisaged the dreadful things that 21st-century broiler-house owners and chicken farmers are prepared to perpetrate on both their customers and their flocks. Chickens were once a luxury here and decent free-range birds (the only kind you should buy) are expensive enough to be considered pretty much a luxury item again – but worth it in terms of taste and peace of mind.

An organic free-range chicken won't be stuffed full of hormones and injected with water, nor will it have spent its life in darkness being cannibalised by its peers. Whatever it costs, it will repay you over and over again, not least because it'll taste so good: roast it, use the leftovers in white sauce, risottos and pilaff, sandwiches and soups, and turn the bones into stock. Poach the breasts and serve the legs and wings cold at picnics or devilled at barbecues.

Poached chicken

The single chicken breast, an object of pathos when it's in the fridge, makes an ideal supper for one. You can turn it into a risotto, roast it with lemon juice in the oven or poach it in wine. I particularly like this last method because it means opening up a bottle without any of the tedious associations of 'drinking by yourself'. You can of course cook an alcohol-free version with just stock or even water. It takes 20 minutes at the most, and to save time you can shove in two or three new potatoes to cook alongside the chicken, which reduces the amount of washing up as well.

Poached chicken

Serves 1

> 1 skinless chicken breast
> ½ bottle dry white wine, or equivalent of
>   half and half wine and chicken stock,
>   or wine and water
> 2 or 3 sprigs of fresh tarragon, chopped
> 2 tablespoons double cream (more if you like)
> sea salt and freshly ground black pepper
> 5 or 6 green peppercorns (optional)

Bring the wine or wine and stock/water mixture plus the peppercorns, if using, to simmering point in a saucepan. Add the chicken breast and half the tarragon and simmer gently for about 15–20 minutes, depending on the size of the breast. Remove the chicken and keep warm. Boil the remaining liquid hard to reduce to about half. Put the cream in a cup or small bowl, stir in a couple of spoonfuls of the cooking liquid, then pour the mixture back into the saucepan and stir. Return the chicken to the pan, add the rest of the tarragon and reheat gently, stirring all the time. Serve with potatoes.

Grilled chicken

JW discovered this recipe in Nigel Slater's *Real Cooking* and has been making it ever since. Handily, he has taught my daughter how to make it too, so this delicious fast chicken supper is pretty much always made by someone other than me. I have a particular fondness for it. Like all Slater's recipes, it combines rich and zingy taste with eminent practicality. Slater says, 'My first choice for [this dish] is the legs from a fat, free-range bird that have had their bones removed to give two near rectangles of flesh. Ask your butcher or have a go yourself...' You can adapt it to suit just about any part of the chicken, however, and I doubt that JW pays any attention to the 'salt flakes' injunction. The smell while you are cooking it is absolutely heavenly.

Grilled chicken with thyme leaves, salt and garlic butter

(from *Real Cooking* by Nigel Slater)

Serves 2

> *2 boned chicken legs (or breasts if you must – NS)*
> *olive oil*
> *1 tablespoon thyme leaves*
> *2 or more juicy cloves of garlic*

about 50 g soft butter
a small handful of chopped parsley
a lemon
sea salt flakes – not crystals

Get a griddle pan hot. This means leaving it for 3 or 4
minutes over the gas burner or electric ring till you can
feel the heat rising from the pan. Meanwhile, rub both
the flesh and skin side of the chicken with a generous
amount of olive oil and the thyme leaves. Put each piece
of chicken, skin down, on the hot grill. It should crackle
and spit. Leave the meat in place for at least 2 minutes.
Press the meat down on the grill with a palette knife or
similar (splutter pop bang). Turn the meat over and cook
for a further 7 or 8 minutes, until cooked through and
golden brown on each side. The flesh should be juicy.
Meanwhile, peel and crush the garlic with the parsley,
butter and juice of the lemon. A pestle and mortar is
good for this. It will take all of 2 minutes. When the
chicken is cooked, crumble over the sea salt and
serve with a dollop of the lemon garlic butter on top.

Poulet à l'estragon
'Tarragon is a herb which has a quite remarkable affinity
with chicken,' wrote Elizabeth David in *French Provincial
Cooking*, 'and a poulet à l'estragon, made with fresh
tarragon, is one of the great treats of the summer.'

'Fresh' is the word to remember here; it's absolutely no good trying to make this wonderful dish without fresh tarragon. David stuffs her chicken with butter, tarragon, garlic, salt and pepper and then, dramatically, pours flaming brandy over the bird to make the sauce.

Rowley Leigh has a relatively restrained version in *No Place Like Home,* which involves stuffing tarragon butter between the skin and the meat of a whole chicken, using a saucepan as well as the roasting tin and eventually jointing the chicken as well. For an easy life, I'd use Sophie Grigson's fail-safe recipe in her book *Meat Course.* It is straightforward and easy to do and always tastes wonderful.

Poulet à l'estragon

(from *Meat Course* by Sophie Grigson)

Serves 4

> 1.75-kg (4-lb) free-range chicken
> ½ lemon
> 4 branches of tarragon
> 50 g (2 oz) unsalted butter
> 50 ml (2 fl oz) vermouth
>   or a small glass of dry white wine
> 300 ml (10 fl oz) crème fraîche or double cream
> lemon juice
> salt and pepper

Preheat the oven to 200°C/400°F/gas mark 6. Rub the skin of the chicken all over with the lemon half and stuff the used lemon half in the stomach cavity of the chicken along with three branches of the tarragon. Chop the leaves of the remaining branch, discarding the stalks. Sit the bird in a roasting tin, smear the butter thickly over its skin and season with salt and pepper. Roast for $1\frac{1}{2}$ hours, until cooked through. Transfer the bird to a serving dish and let it rest in the oven with the heat turned off and the door ajar.

To make the sauce. Skim the fat from the roasting tin, leaving behind the roasting juices. Put the tin on the hob and pour in the vermouth or wine. Bring to the boil, scraping in any residues from roasting and boil until reduced to a few spoonfuls. Add the cream and stir and let it return to the boil. Cook hard until reduced to a good consistency. Draw off the heat and add 2–3 teaspoons of the chopped tarragon. Season with salt and pepper and a dash of lemon juice. Serve the sauce with the chicken.

You can turn a couple of old chicken breasts or legs (assuming they haven't been skinned) into something impressive by making either Rowley Leigh's tarragon butter stuffing (mix together butter, tarragon leaves, a chopped shallot and $\frac{1}{2}$ teaspoon of coarse ground black pepper) or a basil butter (substitute basil for the

the tarragon and leave out the shallot) and stuffing
it between the skin and meat. Roast in a hot oven
for 20–30 minutes, or until done, and serve with a salad
(a tomato one in the case of the basil butter – chopped
tomatoes and basil, sea salt, ground black pepper,
drizzled with olive oil and a dash of balsamic vinegar).

Chicken in cabbage

The recipe that rather puts the kibosh on the idea that
you can improvise and adapt with different ingredients
is Alastair Little's Wrapped Breast of Chicken with Wild
Mushrooms. It was a signature dish at his eponymous

restaurant – 'a genuinely original dish,' as he describes
it, 'something a chef can rarely say' – and depends on
having exactly what he says in the recipe. JW, who has
cooked it often and successfully in London, found this
out by attempting to reproduce it while staying near
Galway in the western extremity of Ireland. He described
the experience in his book *Falling Angels.* He set off
to Quinnsworth's supermarket with a list: But there
wasn't any Savoy cabbage ('there's some perfectly nice
ordinary cabbage over there,' the girl said); there weren't
any shallots ('but the onions over there are pretty small,'
the girl reasoned); there weren't any ceps or morels
('but the button mushrooms will do fine, I'd say,' the
girl confided). There wasn't any prosciutto, nor pancetta,
nor any other Italian substitute ('but sure, what's wrong
with good Irish ham?' the girl asked, a little peeved by
now. 'Isn't it all from the pig, one way or the other?').
There were, however, some chicken breasts.

Back home, JW assembled his various purchases and
asked for some foil in which to wrap each chicken breast
in its ham and cabbage shroud as per instructions. 'We
used it all up at Christmas, but perhaps you could wrap
it with some string.' Half an hour later, the dish having
gone into the oven, the smell of roast greens was all
over the house like a gigantic fart and the dish itself a
travesty of charred leaves and ham and raw chicken.

Wrapped breast of chicken with wild mushrooms

(from *Keep it Simple* by Alastair Little)

Serves 4

> *55 g (2 oz) dried morels, soaked in warm water*
> *   for half an hour*
> *30 g (1 oz) dried ceps, soaked in warm water*
> *   for half an hour*
> *225 g (8 oz) butter*
> *2 shallots, peeled and chopped*
> *8 large leaves of Savoy cabbage*
> *   (outer leaves only)*
> *8 slices of pancetta, or 4 of prosciutto*
> *   (cut on no. 2 thickness)*
> *300 ml (½ pint) chicken stock*
> *1 glass (150 ml/¼ pint) dry white wine*
> *4 large chicken supremes*
> *salt and pepper*

Preheat the oven to its highest setting. Generously
butter a roasting dish big enough to hold the 4 chicken
packages. Spread the shallots evenly over the bottom
of the dish. Butter four 20-cm (8-inch) squares of foil.
Blanch the cabbage leaves in boiling salted water for
3 minutes and refresh in cold water. Drain and cut out

chicken and game -
wrapped breast of chicken
with wild mushrooms

the tough bottom part of the stalk from each leaf.
Spread 2 of the green leaves on each foil square to
cover. Place 2 slices of pancetta on top of the leaves,
to cover as much of the green as possible. Place a
15-g (½-oz) piece of butter in the middle and put a
chicken supreme on it. Grind some black pepper over
it. Fold the leaves and ham round the chicken and
roll the foil round it.

Drain the mushroom water into a saucepan through
a fine sieve. Add the chicken stock and white wine
and boil to reduce to 600 ml (1 pint) of liquid. Scatter
the mushrooms over the shallots in the roasting dish.
Arrange the 4 chicken packets in the dish and pour the
hot stock over them. Bake for 30 minutes. Remove from
the oven and transfer the packages to a hot dish and
leave to rest in a warm place. Put the roasting dish on
the hob and bring to a rolling boil and reduce to about
150 ml (¼ pint). Season, whisk in the remaining butter
a piece at a time until amalgamated and then pour into
a gravy dish.

To serve unwrap the chicken from the foil, carve each
supreme into three pieces. Pour the sauce on to 4
heated plates and arrange the slices, overlapping,
in the centre of each plate. Serve immediately.

Pheasant

'To the uninitiated this bird is a sealed book' – Anon

Unless you have a large estate, are a member of a rough shoot or live near a good butcher, it's surprisingly hard to find a decent pheasant at short notice. You wouldn't think the whole of the UK beyond the South Circular Road is crawling with them. They turn up in the most unexpected places, though not nearly often enough in your local supermarket.

Mrs Beeton thought a pheasant is such a 'dry bird', you should stick a quarter of a pound of beefsteak inside it to moisten it. She also advocated leaving the head on. It's true that roasting it can end in disaster, and to my mind nothing beats pheasant casseroled with calvados, apples and cream. It's surprisingly easy to assemble, even when you're staying in the depths of the countryside.

In Faisan à la Cauchoise, Elizabeth David cooks the pheasant and apple apart. She browns a roasting pheasant in butter in a heavy iron pan on top of the stove, then pouring in a warmed glass of calvados (or brandy), setting light to it and, when the flames have burnt out, adding 'a good measure' of thick cream. She serves separately a little dish of diced sweet apple, fried in butter and kept warm in the oven (2 apples will be sufficient for 1 pheasant). Her recipe is found in *French Provincial Cooking*. It works just as well if you fry the onions and apple together, and add the wine and cream to make the sauce. But the pheasant recipe I like best is from my Aunt Dot, the person who introduced me to pheasant in the first place. It was printed on a postcard she sent me from France.

Recette du faisan au cidre

Serves 4

> *1 pheasant, weighing roughly 1.5 kg*
> *2–3 shallots, chopped*
> *2 carrots, chopped*
> *3 dl calvados (or armagnac)*
> *½ glass dry cider*
> *1 dl of crème fraîche*
> *olive oil*

Preheat the oven to 180°C/350°F/gas mark 4. Brown the pheasant on all sides in a frying pan. In an ovenproof casserole put the chopped shallots and the carrot and lay the pheasant, breast side up, on top and leave to one side to keep warm. Put the frying pan back on the heat and deglaze with the calvados. Bring to the boil and add the cider. Leave it to simmer for about 5 minutes, then add the crème fraîche. Reduce for 2–3 minutes and then pour the sauce over the pheasant and cook in the oven for 45 minutes to an hour. Serve with potatoes.

The most exotic pheasant recipe makes an appearance in *The Cookbook of the United Nations,* first published in the US in 1964, when the UN still had some clout. The book, edited by Barbara Kraus (described in the blurb as 'liaison officer between the UN Association of the USA and the Delegations', and therefore 'the ideal person to undertake such a project') features pages of extraordinary food from countries whose place amongst the brotherhood of nations is tenuous, to say the least – Leek Ravioli from Afghanistan, 'Plate National' (beans, parsley, bacon and rice) from Haiti, Chicken Peanut Soup from Liberia and Cucumber Cocktail from Albania. This' is Georgian Pheasant. You can substitute bacon for salt pork and I've also made it with almonds, though it's better with walnuts. I've never bothered to brown the

flour and you can make the sauce by adding cream
instead of the flour and butter mixture.

Georgian pheasant

(from *The Cookbook of the United Nations*)

Serves 4–6

> 2½ lb pheasant
> 6 thin slices of salt pork
> 6 oz walnuts, coarsely chopped
> 1½ lb white seedless grapes, chopped
> ½ pint orange juice
> ¼ pint Muscat wine
> ¼ pint strong Georgian tea
> 1½ oz flour, browned in oven
> 2 oz butter
> salt and pepper

Preheat the oven to 170°C/325°F/gas mark 3. Rub
the inside of the pheasant with salt and pepper. Skewer
the slices of salt pork over the breast and place in a
large casserole. Add the walnuts, grapes, orange juice,
wine and tea. Cover and cook for 1½ hours in a very
moderate oven. When done, remove the pheasant from

the casserole and place in a shallow baking dish. Remove the salt pork and return the pheasant to the oven to brown.

To make the sauce, mix the flour and butter to a smooth paste, stir in 6 tablespoons of the liquid in which the pheasant was cooked. Blend and add to the remaining liquid in the casserole. Cook and stir until the sauce is thickened. Serve the sauce with the pheasant.

Duck

'The ducks were raised in the abodes of the cottagers. Round the walls of the living rooms ... are fixed rows of wooden boxes, lined with hay; and it is the business of the wife and children to nurse and comfort the feathered lodgers, to feed the little ducklings, and to take the old ones out for an airing' – Mrs Beeton, on the duck breeders of Buckinghamshire, 1861

As Ogden Nash once wrote, there are many ways to catch a duck ('This grown-up man with pluck and luck is hoping to outwit a duck...') and, having got your duck, there are just as many ways to cook it. Welsh salt duck (1867), according to Elizabeth David in her *Spices, Salt and Aromatics in the English Kitchen,* bears some resemblance to Nanking fresh salted duck: 'In the original,' she writes, 'the duck was eaten hot, with an onion sauce, which would have been rather heavy'; in France, you can enjoy canard à l'orange, or with turnips; in Poland, duck and red cabbage; in Iran, you get fesenjan, braised duck with walnut and pomegranate sauce. In England, we roast it with apple sauce, or stew it with peas à la Hannah Glasse, whose 18th-century recipe is still useful today, descended via the interpretive hands of Elizabeth David, Elisabeth Ayrton, Jane and Sophie Grigson.

Duck stewed with green peas

(Hannah Glasse, from *The Cookery of England*
by Elisabeth Ayrton)

Serves 3

> 1 duck
> 360 g (½ lb) shelled fresh peas
>   (or 2 large packets of frozen peas)
> 1 small onion, finely chopped
> 3 dl (½ pint) good stock
> 1 lettuce, cut up fairly finely
> 90 g (3 oz) butter
> a little flour for thickening
> sprigs of thyme, marjoram, parsley and mint
> 1 dl (3 oz) double cream
> pepper and salt
> 1 saltspoon each of ground mace and nutmeg
> 12 croutons of fried bread

Rub the duck with flour, salt and pepper. Melt 60 g (2 oz)
butter in a deep saucepan and brown the bird all over.
Pour off all the fat, and put in the stock, onion, peas,
lettuce, herbs, salt and pepper. Closely cover and stew
gently for 35 minutes. Shake or stir the peas lightly from

time to time. After 35 minutes, stir in the mace and
nutmeg, cook for 1 minute, add 30 g (1 oz) of butter
into which you have worked a dessertspoon of flour,
stir well and add the cream. Place the duck on a hot
dish, remove the herbs and pour the peas and gravy
all round. Surround with croutons and serve very hot.

Hannah Glasse's cooking times are short compared
to Jane Grigson. Ms Grigson browns the duck in oil,
and then places it breast down in a deep pot with ½ pint
of stock, covers and simmers it for 1¼ hours. Once that
has been done, turn the duck over, add 1 lb shelled
peas, a shredded lettuce and simmer for a further 45
minutes. To make the sauce, remove the duck and the
lettuce and keep them warm. Boil the remaining liquid
hard. Mix 2 egg yolks and 4 tablespoons double cream
in a bowl and pour on about half the stock, whisking
well. Return this mixture to the cooking pot and stir
over a low heat, not allowing it to come to the boil.
Finish with a dash of lemon juice and season. Pour
over the duck and lettuce and serve at once. She
doesn't bother with the croutons, and neither would I.
(Grigson's recipe serves 4—5, slightly more than
the curious threesome catered for by Hannah Glasse.)

Duck pilaf

This is a Simon Hopkinson recipe which appeared in
the *Independent* Magazine some years ago. He calls
it a pilaf because 'the end result of this particular pulse
[moong dhal], once cooked, seems so redolent of a pot
of savoury rice that to call it "baked duck with dahl,
lemon and mint" would fail to attract even the most
informed fans of the farinaceous.' Once he has rolled
out that quite staggeringly pretentious sentence,
Hopkinson goes on to explain that moong dhal is a seed
'possessed with such lightness of starch that it can even
display some of the characteristics of a fine biriyani –
though the traditional Pakistani cook would passionately
disagree with me.'

Well, the description of this recipe is best left to simmer
away by itself, but the minute I saw the accompanying
picture (by Jason Lowe), I wanted to cook this dish, and
have been doing so, with many variations, ever since.
It makes a brilliant quick lunch or a luscious supper
and it's endlessly forbearing about lack of/changes in
ingredients. I have made it with lentils, chicken, leftover
turkey, with rice, with a vegetable stock cube and once
with a lemon so old that the rind would only come off
in rock-hard slices. Such versatility is, I think, the mark
of a seriously good recipe.

chicken and game -
fragrant duck pilaf
with lemon and mint

Fragrant duck pilaf with lemon and mint

(Simon Hopkinson, from the *Independent* Magazine)

Serves 2

4 duck legs
salt and pepper
a litle oil or duck fat
1 large onion, finely chopped
4 cloves of garlic, sliced
1 scant teaspoon of ground cumin
a healthy pinch of dried chilli flakes
350 g moong dhal, rinsed and drained
40 g butter
500 ml good chicken or duck stock
the thinly pared pithless rind of a small lemon
2 tablespoons freshly chopped mint
1 lemon, cut in half, to squeeze over the
    finished dish

Preheat the oven to 180°C/350°F/gas mark 4. Season
the duck legs and using a lidded, flameproof, ovenproof
pot, gently fry the duck in the oil or fat, skin side down
until golden and crisp. Then turn them over and lightly
colour the other sides. Remove to a plate.

Discard all but 2 tablespoons of the rendered fat, and add the onions and garlic. Gently fry until pale golden and then stir in the cumin and chilli. Add the butter and then stir around for a little longer before tipping in the dhal. Coat the grains with fat, using a stirring and folding motion, until all are glistening. Pour in the stock all at once, bring to a simmer and stir in the lemon rind and mint. Cut the duck legs in half, through their natural joints and slide into the mixture along with any of their exuded juices. Put on the lid and bake in the oven for 30 minutes. Remove, but leave the lid on for a further 10 minutes before having a look. Lift off the lid, fluff up the grains with a fork and serve at once with the lemon halves alongside.

You can make a version of pilaf with pheasant, almonds and pomegranate seeds. Scattered with coriander, and piled on a vast earthenware dish, this looks like Christmas on a plate and is a recipe by Rose Prince which originally appeared in the *Spectator*. And in *Mediterranean Food*, Elizabeth David has 'one of the most comforting dishes imaginable' – namely Suliman's Pilaff – in which she mixes 2 cupfuls of rice fried in oil and boiled hard in roughly 4 pints of water with a 'savoury preparation of small pieces of cooked mutton, fried onions, raisins, currants, garlic, tomatoes and pine

nuts all sautéd in dripping with plenty of seasoning'.
Put the cooked rice into a pan and stir in the meat
and onion mixture, heat over a low flame and serve
with sour cream or yogurt.

I have added lots more garlic, and grated ginger, parsley
and chopped chestnuts to this. It makes the perfect
Monday night supper.

Grouse

Grouse is in season from 12 August to 10 December,
the Glorious Twelfth being the occasion that brings out,
as Alan Davidson puts it, 'the sub-species of the human
race which [on the grouse moors] is the chief predator of
the grouse and used to be readily recognisable, whether
male or accompanying female, by its raiment of heathery
tweed'. After this sideswipe at the shooting classes,
Davidson admits that grouse are 'excellent to eat ... in
general a recipe that is good for pheasant will suit grouse
too.' He notes that Eliza Acton in 1855 advised that when
a grouse is being roasted, 'a buttered toast should be
introduced under the bird in the dripping pan about ten
minutes before roasting is complete' which 'will afford
a superior relish even to the birds themselves'.

The *WAGBI Game Cookbook* has one of the most straightforward recipes for roast grouse: knead salt, pepper and lemon juice into 1 oz butter and put it inside the bird. Tie a rasher of fat bacon round the bird and roast in a hot oven for 25 minutes. Serve with fried breadcrumbs. Elisabeth Ayrton's Special Roast Grouse adds the all-important toast.

Special roast grouse

(from *The Cookery of England* by Elisabeth Ayrton)

Serves 1–2

> *1 grouse*
> *flour*
> *strips of bacon*

sprig of thyme
round of toast
butter
salt and pepper

Rub the bird all over with salt and pepper and a very
little flour. Wrap a rasher of bacon round the breast.
Put a sprig of thyme and a lump of butter inside the
bird and set it on a large thin piece of toast. Spread
60 g (2 oz) softened butter over it and roast in a very
hot oven for 15–20 minutes according to size.
Grouse should be served slightly underdone.

Serve it whole on the toast, or carve it. Chop the meat
off the legs and mix with a little gravy. Save the grouse
liver, fry it slightly, mix with the chopped legs and gravy
and spread the whole on the toast on which the bird
cooked. Place the carved breast on this and serve.

Elisabeth Ayrton notes that a recipe devised by Sarah
Clayton in 1730, 'Sauce for all sorts of wild fowls',
is a good alternative to gravy. This is her version
of Clayton's original.

½ pint claret or other red wine
½ pint strong brown stock

2 strips of anchovy

12 peppercorns

1 shallot or 1 small onion, chopped

1 oz butter

1 dessertspoon flour

Simmer the red wine and stock, the shallot, anchovy and peppercorns for 1–1½ hours, adding more wine or water if necessary. Strain. Work the flour into the butter and stir into the gravy, beating well to avoid lumps. Serve separately with the birds.

Fish

*'A Red Herring doth nourish little, and is hard of
concoction, but very good to make a cup of good
drink relish well, and may well be called
The Drunkard' s Delight'* – Dr Harte, 1633

*'Into a stockpot he eases the skeletons of three skates.
Their heads are intact, their lips girlishly full. Their eyes
go cloudy on contact with the boiling water ... From the
green string bag of mussels Henry takes a dozen or so
and drops them in with the skate ... the juice of the
tomatoes is simmering with the onions and the rest,
and turning reddish-orange with the saffron'* –
Ian McEwan, *Saturday*

'Avoid fish that have been written on' is a handy hint on
buying a fish supper. It comes courtesy of Ziggy Zen's
book *How to Drink Wine out of Fish Heads while Cooking
Lobster in a Volkswagen Hub Cap.* Firm fins, shiny
scales, protruding eyes and a fresh smell are also useful
pointers. Ziggy's Easy Seafood recipes are not the thing
to try if you are a novice in pescatorial cookery. For that
you need something more down-to-earth, like *Cordon
Bleu Fish* or Darina Allen's cookery bible *Ballymaloe*

Cookery Course. Never undertake a bouillabaisse unless you live in Marseilles and have about a year to spare – it takes forever and will never taste the same on a rainy day in Manchester. As Alice Thomas Ellis puts it in *Fish, Flesh and Good Red Herring:* 'You need the hot sun of Provence, the exuberant and voluble waiter, the Marseillais, bubbling with enthusiasm over his famous local dish...'

The easiest fish to cook are: a whole salmon; any fillets wrapped up in foil with a sprig of dill, a little olive oil and lemon juice, a screw of pepper and baked in the oven; prawns; and fish pie.

Fish pie

Fish pie, like shepherd's pie, will cause virulent
arguments about what does or doesn't go in. Frankly,
it depends where (and how) you were brought up. No
one who spent their childhood eating a fish pie that
consists of plain white fish and boiled eggs in a white
sauce is ever going to believe that inserting prawns or
flaked salmon is going to be a Good Thing. Claire
MacDonald's fish pie is the one that's worked best for
me, a non-controversial combination of the effects of
a puritan childhood and the extravagance of later life.
It's even eaten by small children if you emphasise the
pie, rather than the fish aspect. I leave out the cheese,
but that's purely a personal preference, and I have
from time to time added prawns and scallops and
a dash of white wine when a slightly more glamorous
pie was called for.

This recipe was devised long before we became
embroiled in fishing-stock arguments, so mix and match
the fish to suit your politics. You can also, according
to Lady Macdonald, substitute puff pastry for mash,
but that's a whole different kettle of fish altogether.

Fish pie

(from *Delicious Fish* by Claire MacDonald)

Serves 6–8

> 700 g (1½ lb) haddock, cod or other white fish
> 700 g (1½ lb) smoked haddock or cod
> 1.1 litres (2 pints) milk
> 1 onion, skinned
> 1 blade of mace, optional
> 75 g (3 oz) butter
> 75 g (3 oz) plain flour
> 50 g (2 oz) Cheddar or Lancashire cheese, grated
> 3 tomatoes, skinned, seeded and chopped
> salt and pepper
> 2 hard-boiled eggs, shelled and chopped
> 2 rounded tablespoons finely chopped parsley
> about 900 g (2 lb) potatoes, freshly boiled
>   and mashed

Put the fish, milk, onion and mace together in a saucepan and, over a gentle heat, bring slowly to the boil. Simmer for 2 minutes, then remove the pan from the heat and let the fish cool in the milk. Strain off the milk, when cool, keeping it in a jug to make the sauce. Flake the fish, removing the bones and skin.

Melt the butter in a saucepan and stir in the flour.
Cook for a minute or two, stirring all the time, then
gradually pour on the reserved milk, stirring all the time
until it boils. Take it off the heat and stir in the cheese,
the fish, the hard-boiled eggs and the tomatoes. Season
with a little salt and lots of pepper. Pour all this into
a 2.3-litre (4-pint) ovenproof dish and leave.

Arrange the mash on top and bake in a moderate oven
(180°C/350°F/gas mark 4) for about 40 minutes, until
the sauce under the potato is bubbling and a golden
crust has formed on top.

Fish curry

A classic Goan fish curry was served on P&O's cruise
ship *Chusan* as she steamed across the Indian Ocean
towards Australia in January 1961, a quieter voyage
than the *Chusan's* Atlantic crossing later that decade
when all the babies and toddlers on board seem to
have spent the trip confined to the playpen – 'the only
safe place for them in the Atlantic gales and high seas'.
On the *Chusan*, Goan fish curry (a seductive mix
of fish, coconut milk and spices) is a complex affair,
but I came across a recipe that simplifies the mixture

while retaining its delicious flavour. I found it on the back of a supermarket recipe card which I've kept handy in a box of disintegrating recipe cuttings. Having worked once, these recipes turn into staples, adapted to suit any occasion. This is one of Waitrose's and came in a series called 'Cooking round the world 3' – third series, third recipe or third world? Who knows, but its simplicity and speedy cooking time (ten minutes or so), not to mention its surprisingly authentic taste, make it a classic. Add more chilli if you like it hotter.

Goan fish curry

(from Waitrose)

Serves 4

> 30 ml (2 tablespoons) tikka masala paste
> 1 x 400-g tin of coconut milk
> 5 ml (1 teaspoon) chilli spice
>   or 1 red chilli, chopped
> 2 bay leaves
> 450 g (1 lb) haddock fillets,
>   skinned and cut into 2.5-cm (1-inch) cubes
> 1 red pepper, cored, deseeded and sliced
> 10 ml (2 teaspoons) lemon juice

15 ml (1 tablespoon) cider vinegar
10 ml (2 teaspoons) caster sugar
salt and pepper

Put the tikka paste, coconut milk, chilli and bay leaves
in a saucepan. Bring to the boil, cover and simmer for
5 minutes. Stir in the fish and red pepper. Cover and
simmer for a further 5–6 minutes or until the fish is
just cooked. Gently stir in the lemon juice, vinegar
and sugar and season to taste. Serve with bowls
of steamed basmati rice.

Kedgeree

Two kedgerees stick in my mind. One was made by the
owner of a B&B in Cheltenham who had obviously spent
years perfecting the skill on the Anglo-Irish punters who
flood into the town every year for the Gold Cup – it was
part of the Platonic ideal of a country-house breakfast,
complete with chafing dishes, cream, eggs and salmon.
The other was at Chutney Mary in the Kings Road and
was the complete reverse – hot, spicy and foreign.
I have realised while researching this book that the
kedgeree I have been making over the years, inflicting
on my children and hungover New Year's Day guests,

is a mongrel version, a subconscious amalgamation of the two. (I must have made it up.) Its main advantage is that it's quick and easy and it tastes pretty good. The disadvantage is the pong of boiling fish. Open the windows before you start.

Start with a couple of fillets of smoked haddock or cod and poach in barely boiling water for 10 minutes. Drain, reserving the water, and flake and debone the fish. In a frying pan, fry a chopped onion in oil, add a teaspoon or two of curry powder, cook for a minute or so and add roughly 175 g (6 oz) of rice. Stir for a further couple of minutes and then slowly add the water in which the fish was cooked. Add the flaked fish, and prawns if you have them, a handful of chopped parsley and stir from time to time, adding more liquid if necessary until the rice is cooked. You can then add, if you feel like it, a couple of chopped boiled eggs and a further scattering of chopped parsley. Serve immediately. This amount should do for four to six people. Any leftovers should be heated up in the oven with a knob or two of butter and spread on buttered toast for supper – possibly the best supper you'll ever have.

Mark Hix has a proper, posh version of this colonial leftover, noting its peasant origins – 'the Hindi rice,

lentil and onion dish of khichri was developed from
the peasant meal by the British in India as a good way
of using up fish and rice.' Hix thinks smoked Finnan
haddock makes the best kedgeree 'by far. Don't be
tempted to buy bright, yellow, dyed haddock fillet:
no smoke on this earth has ever been known to produce
that colour. A few prawns make a luxurious addition.'

Kedgeree

(from *Fish* by Mark Hix)

Serves 4

> *150 g basmati rice*
> *200 g natural smoked haddock fillet,*
>   *bones removed and lightly poached*
> *150 g salmon fillet, skinned,*
>   *boned and lightly poached*
> *3 eggs, hard-boiled, shelled and chopped*
> *lime or lemon wedges to serve*
> *For the curry sauce:*
> *30 g butter*
> *1 large onion, finely chopped*
> *1 garlic clove, crushed*
> *2 teaspoons finely chopped root ginger*

$1/2$ teaspoon ground turmeric
$1/2$ teaspoon ground cumin
$1/2$ teaspoon curry powder
$1/2$ teaspoon fenugreek seeds, crushed
a good pinch of saffron threads
100 ml fish stock
200 ml double cream
salt and pepper
2 tablespoons chopped coriander

To make the sauce: melt the butter in a heavy-based
pan and gently cook the onion, garlic and ginger without
allowing them to colour. Add all the spices and cook
for another minute to release the flavours. Add the fish
stock, bring to the boil and allow to reduce by half.
Pour in the cream and simmer gently for 15 minutes.
Blend the sauce in a liquidiser until smooth, then strain
through a fine-meshed sieve. Adjust the seasoning.
Meanwhile cook the rice for about 12–15 minutes,
drain and return to the pan off the heat with a lid on.

To serve: reheat the curry sauce and add the cooked
smoked haddock, salmon and coriander. Put the rice
into a bowl, spoon over the fish and sauce, then scatter
over the eggs. Serve with lime or lemon wedges.

Scallops

'Best caught by divers and sold in the shell when still
alive,' says Rowley Leigh, proprietor of Kensington Place
and the Fish Shop at Kensington Place (tel: 0207 243
6626). If you don't have a friendly diver to hand, look
for scallops that haven't been soaked in water to
increase their weight (they'll be puffed up and white),
but which are fresh and unsoaked and therefore
a pearly, opalescent colour and very firm. Having
once discovered scallops and pea purée on the menu
at Kensington Place, I find it hard to resist them
whenever I go there. They appear in Leigh's cookbook,
No Place Like Home.

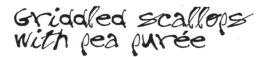

Griddled scallops with pea purée

(from *No Place Like Home* by Rowley Leigh)

Serves 2

> *2 spring onions*
> *butter*
> *outside leaves of a lettuce*
> *150 g fresh shelled or frozen peas*

1 bunch of mint

nutmeg

sugar

½ glass white wine

75 ml double cream

lemon juice

50 ml cider vinegar or white wine vinegar

125 ml sunflower oil

8 scallops, shucked,

   rinsed and cut in half if very large

To make the purée: slice the spring onions and stew
them in a little butter. Finely shred the lettuce leaves
and add them to the pan, then stir in the peas.
Add 3 or 4 leaves of mint, a small pinch of nutmeg,
a good pinch of sugar, and some salt and pepper.
Add the white wine and then stew, covered, on a low
heat for half an hour. When the peas are very tender
and swollen, add the cream and simmer briskly to
reduce, until it is in danger of catching on the sides of
the pan. Remove from the heat and purée in a blender
until very smooth. Season with lemon, salt and pepper.
Put the purée in a small saucepan and keep warm.

To cook the scallops: salt the scallops lightly, leave
them for 10 minutes and then pat dry with kitchen

paper. Lightly brush them with a little sunflower oil.
Get a heavy, dry frying pan or a griddle very hot and
put the scallops in it one by one. Do not move them for
a couple of minutes but let them brown well. Turn and
cook for another 2 minutes, then remove. They should
be very hot in the middle, but very moist. To serve,
arrange the scallops round a mound of the pea purée
on each plate. Don't drown the scallops.

Scallops with black pudding

The combination of scallops and black pudding is
curiously delicious, and although you'd think it'd be
impossible to do within the confines of your own home –
there's something about a scallop that puts the amateur
chef into a spin – it's strangely simple. As with most
minimalist dishes, it's the quality of the ingredients that
counts. Buy really fresh scallops with the corals intact,
and the best black pudding you can find. For this dish,
the texture of the pudding is important. It shouldn't be
too soft – a Spanish morcilla is ideal.

In my less-than-perfect homemade version of this
recipe, I sear the seasoned scallops (reckon three small
scallops per person for a starter) in a lightly oiled pan

over a highish flame for a minute or two on each side, remove and keep warm, then fry the same number of slices of black pudding (roughly 1 cm/½ inch thick) in the same pan for about the same amount of time on each side. Put a small collection of herby leaves, preferably just gathered from the garden, or what you happen to have in the fridge, on each plate and stack the scallops and black pudding alternately on top. It looks spectacular, takes about six minutes to do and makes a wonderful starter.

There are more sophisticated versions of this recipe, one of which is by Mark Hix, chef director of J. Sheekey, and possibly the only man, other than Rick Stein and Alan Davidson, you need consult when it comes to cooking fish.

Scallops with black pudding, girolles and mousseline potato

(from *Fish* by Mark Hix)

Serves 4

120 g butter
1 small garlic clove, crushed

125 g small girolle mushrooms, wiped

salt and pepper

1 tablespoon chopped parsley

12 medium-size scallops, with corals,
    rinsed and patted dry

12 slices of black pudding, each about 1 cm thick

200 g floury potato, peeled, cooked and mashed

3 tablespoons double cream

Melt 80 g of the butter in a frying pan until it foams
(don't let it go brown). Add the garlic and the girolles,
season with salt and pepper and cook gently for 2–3
minutes until they begin to soften. Add the parsley and
remove from the heat. Meanwhile, lightly oil a non-stick
frying pan and heat it over a medium to high flame.
Season the scallops with salt and pepper and cook for
a minute on each side. Remove from the pan and keep
warm, then cook the black pudding for about a minute
again on each side.

Meanwhile, heat the mashed potato through, remove from
the heat, stir in the remaining butter and the cream and
season. The potato should be a thick sauce-like consistency
and spoonable. To serve, spoon the potato flat on warmed
plates, arrange layers of the scallops and black pudding on
the potato and arrange the girolles and butter on top.

Prawns and shrimps

Prawns with mustard and coriander

Sainsbury's, I think – it seems way back in the mists of last-century life now – once ran an advertising campaign in which a well-known cook created a succulent dish in the time it took you to change channels. The emphasis was purely on speed, and the results were duly published in a series of recipe cards introduced by the words 'Simply take ...' Prawns with Mustard and Coriander was one of them, a surprisingly successful dish which you can indeed cook in five minutes, as they boast (though you have to remember to get the rice going in advance), and therefore perfect for those fraught post-work, not-back-until-8 pm-and-shattered days when you want something more exciting than a leftover fishfinger and half a tomato.

Prawns with mustard and coriander

(from Sainsbury's)

Serves 4

> 25 g (1 oz) butter
> 2 teaspoons sesame oil

2 sticks of celery, chopped
1 clove of garlic, crushed
500 g (1 lb) frozen, defrosted and drained,
    or fresh prawns
3 tablespoons fish stock
3 teaspoons Dijon mustard
2 tablespoons medium dry sherry
1½ level teaspoons cornflour
142-ml (5-fl oz) carton of double cream
ground pepper
1–2 tablespoons coriander, chopped

Heat the butter and oil in a pan. Add the celery, garlic
and prawns and stir-fry for 1 minute. Add the fish stock,
mustard and sherry. Blend the cornflour with a little water
and stir in. Bring to the boil and add the cream and black
pepper. Sprinkle over the coriander. Serve with rice.

Rereading this recipe, I realised that I've never included
the cornflour as I could never see what it was doing
there. It seemed needlessly to complicate matters and
the dish works just as well without. I probably used olive
oil instead of sesame oil, having more of the former to
hand. In extremis, you can make a perfectly adequate
fish stock by swilling out the packet in which the prawns
arrived with a bit of water and leftover white wine.
As you can see, it's an extremely versatile recipe,
with surprisingly sophisticated results.

Potted shrimps

In her *Daily Telegraph* column, Rose Prince outlined the technique: 'Potting is based on an ancient method of preserving that involves packing cooked seafood, game, poultry or meat into a pot to exclude air, then covering it with a layer of clarified butter. You need only use a small amount of fat and providing you use good farmhouse butter, it will be pleasantly unctuous, melting deliciously if spread on hot toast.'

Put like that, it's hard to resist, and often just the thing after a hard day's work, especially as you can make it up to three days in advance and keep it in the fridge.

All you need to do when you get home is make the toast. Although you can also pot prawns, the ones you really want for that authentic gentleman's-club taste are the tiny brown shrimps from Morecambe Bay.

Mark Hix's recipe in *Fish* is a masterpiece of simplicity: Melt 175 g unsalted butter in a pan, add lemon juice, mace or nutmeg, bay leaf, cayenne pepper, anchovy essence or paste and simmer gently on a very low heat for 2 minutes. Remove from heat and keep warm. Add 200 g peeled brown shrimps, stir and season and put the mixture in the fridge. When it starts to set, fill 4 ramekins. Serve with warm toast.

It bears some resemblance to the 19th-century recipe devised by Betsy Tatterstall and described in Elisabeth Ayrton's *The Cookery of England*: 'A solid potful of shrimps cemented together with a soft pink butter. It was a great delicacy, and always served on fine white china.'

Neither, however, really looks like one's idea of the classic potted shrimp – for that you need this 18th-century recipe which came from a Suffolk manor house, slightly adapted for modern-day use. You can also use it with lobsters, crabs and crayfish.

Potted shrimps

450 g (1 lb) shelled shrimps or prawns
225 g (8 oz) clarified butter
1 bay leaf
1 teaspoon freshly grated nutmeg or mace
$\frac{1}{2}$ teaspoon powdered ginger
salt and pepper
cayenne pepper

Mix the prawns or shrimps together with the mace and ginger, and season (I'd use sea salt and freshly ground pepper). To clarify the butter, put it in a small saucepan and heat slowly to boiling point. Let it bubble for a few seconds, then strain through a sieve lined with butter muslin, into a bowl. Leave to cool, and then chill until set. When it's set, put 175 g (6 oz) of the butter in a bowl set over a pan of simmering water. Add the bay leaf and season with salt and pepper. When melted stir in the shrimp mixture and amalgamate well. Leave over the heat for 10 minutes, stirring occasionally. Discard the bay leaf and spoon the shrimp mixture into a dish or individual ramekins and press down.

Melt the remaining butter and pour over the tops of the ramekins while the mixture is still hot. The shrimps should be just covered by the butter. Leave to cool and then chill in the fridge. Serve sprinkled with cayenne pepper with hot toast.

Mussels

The oyster beds of the Charente Maritime on the west coast of France have a rich tradition of al fresco shellfish cookery. Mussels baked in pine needles seems to be the epitome of a carefree, seaside existence that mostly one can only dream about. This regional recipe works in a suburban back garden too, though you'll have to imagine the sound of the Atlantic rollers crashing in and the plaintive cries of seabirds. If you do try this, make sure you have a plentiful supply of chilled

Pineau des Charentes and a bucket of water in case of emergencies. It makes an excellent way of using up a dead Christmas tree.

Eclade des moules à la Charentais

Serves 4 (cook outside)

> *2 kg (4½ lb) fresh mussels*
> *45 x 30-cm (18 x 12-inch) plank of wood*
> *a large basket of dried pine needles*
> *matches*

Dip the plank in salt or fresh water. Put it on a fireproof piece of ground or flat surface (do not lay it across a plastic bucket). Lay four mussels in a cross on the centre of the plank, hinges up, fat ends facing the centre. Wedge a circle of mussels round the cross (always hinges up, fat end pointing to the centre). Interlace the remaining mussels as above until the plank is full. Cover the mussels with a thick layer of pine needles and set alight. When the flames have almost died out add an additional layer of pine needles. Continue adding needles in small batches until the mussels have opened. Blow off the ashes and serve on the plank with bread, salted butter and glasses of chilled Pineau.

Squid

The famous dish of grilled squid with chillies served up
at the River Café in London is really all you need to know
about cooking this particular shell-less mollusc. When
Hugh Fearnley-Whittingstall was learning his trade at the
River Café, he ate it every day. It's one of those fantastically
simple combinations (squid, chilli, olive oil, rocket leaves,
salt and pepper) that pretty much makes itself – chop the
chilli, douse it in oil and spoon over the squid which has
been seasoned and grilled for 2–3 minutes.

Cook squid either very fast, or very slow. If you hanker
after the crispy squid dished up in smart Corfiot
restaurants or avant-garde oriental eateries then
this is the recipe to follow.

Crispy squid

(Rose Prince, from *The Daily Telegraph*)

The trick is to fry the squid twice in a fat with a high smoking point. Groundnut (peanut) oil is best.

Always buy fresh squid – and choose larger ones over hard-to-clean baby squid. Reckon 1–2 squid per person. Cut them open lengthways and scrape away the insides including the hard quill. Snip off the tentacles, removing the hard ball of bone in their centre. Dab the squid dry with paper towels. Use a sharp knife to score the flesh on one side, making a lattice pattern, then cut into bite-sized pieces.

Line a large colander with kitchen paper and set it over a bowl. Pour groundnut oil into a wok to about 4 cm deep and heat until it sizzles when a tiny globule of water is dropped into it – at arm's length. Dip each piece of squid in flour, including the tentacles, then fry in small batches for 2 minutes. Remove to the paper-lined sieve and cool.

Just before you eat, reheat the oil. Fry the squid a second time – for about 3–4 minutes or until pale golden. Lift out, drain on clean kitchen paper – the squid will stay warm for some time. Season with sea salt and fresh ground black pepper and serve with a sweet chilli dipping sauce. If you pass an oriental supermarket, ask if they have any old newspapers printed in Chinese or another South East Asian script. Shape sheets of it into small cones to serve your crispy squid at parties.

Tuna

I discovered this stunning, simple recipe while staying in Dubai. It is the brainchild of Michael Goodman, the young American chef who runs Napa restaurant at the Al Qasr hotel. It takes about two minutes to make, looks spectacularly swish for a dinner party and tastes wonderful. You do have to search out sashimi-grade tuna, however or it won't work.

Tuna tartare

(Michael Goodman)

Serves 2–4

> 250 g sashimi-grade tuna
> 1 shallot, chopped finely
> zest of half a lemon, grated
> dash of Thai fish sauce

a bunch of chopped chives
1 small tomato, skinned and seeded and diced
2 or 3 capers, crushed
1 tablespoon aioli
salt and pepper

Dice the tuna finely, removing any sinew, and mix well with all the remaining ingredients. Adjust the seasoning to taste. Serve chilled, piled in little mounds on the plate, with a small amount of salad.

Salmon

'When the Albertine rose is just coming into bud I tend to think, poetically, Poached Salmon. This has something to do with the appearance of the rose – shades of pink, petals/flakes – and something to do with the time of year. When summer starts, you feel you can serve cold food with a clear conscience' – Alice Thomas Ellis

It's become a bit of a cliché because of its associations with June weddings and 21st birthday parties, but poached salmon is one of the most delicious summer lunches. It pretty much cooks itself, though you need a couple of pints of court bouillon and a fish kettle to do it properly. Serve it cold with new potatoes in butter, sliced cucumbers and mayonnaise.

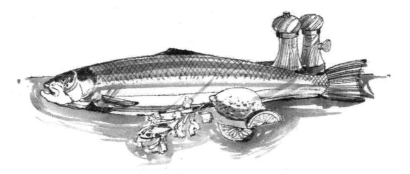

Poached salmon

(from *Leith's Cookery Bible*
by Prue Leith and Caroline Waldegrave)

Serves 4–6

  1 whole salmon
     or large piece of fish (1.5 kg/3–3½ lb)
For the court bouillon:
  1.1 litres (2 pints) water
  1 teaspoon salt
  150 ml (¼ pint) white wine vinegar
  1 onion, sliced
  1 bunch of fresh parsley
  1 sprig of thyme
  1 bay leaf
  6 black peppercorns

Simmer together all the court bouillon ingredients for 1 hour. Strain and cool. Put the fish into the now cold court bouillon and heat gently, bringing up to poaching temperature. Don't simmer or boil, the water should be barely moving. Poach it for 4 minutes. Turn the heat off and leave it to cool – it will finish cooking while it does so. When it's cooked (slightly pink, flaking but still moist), remove it from the court bouillon, put it on a large oval-shaped plate and decorate with the cucumber slices.

If you have any poached salmon left over, you can turn it into fishcakes. Mrs Somerville's *Cookery and Domestic Economy* (1862) minces the 'remains of salmon', mixes it with breadcrumbs, flour, chopped parsley, pepper and salt, and a little curry if you like. 'Bind all together with an egg, and make them up into round balls, or flat cakes and fry them.' In my childhood, fishcakes were always made with leftover mashed potato – usually with a very high ratio of mash to fish – and were extremely stodgy.

My Favourite Recipes for Dainty Dishes, a collection of recipes from the great houses of the north, published in 1896 in aid of the Cripples Home at Gosforth, includes a recipe for Fish Cakes: 1 lb of fish to ½ lb of mashed potato mixed together. Melt 1 oz butter and a tablespoon of milk in a largish pan, add the fish and potato mixture, seasoning and the yolk of an egg. Make the resulting mixture into 12 cakes, dip them in beaten egg and then into breadcrumbs and fry until golden brown. Serve with fried parsley. They sound delicious, though I would add some tarragon to the fish mixture and a lot of ground pepper, extra milk and melted butter too, if it's looking stodgy.

Miscellaneous

Soup

You can make a soup out of anything – boots, sandals, beef stock, carrots, caviar, lobster, elephant trunks, salmon and custard, as was demonstrated by the *Bird's Cookery Book* in the 50s ('First remove the bones and the skin') and even crow, though, as an anonymous 19th-century naturalist once noted, 'The flesh of this bird is repulsive, but it does provide an excellent and very healthy soup.'

Quentin Crisp went one stage further and made a soup out of nothing. His Tibetan Workhouse Soup ('Take a saucepan which has been used for a variety of purposes

without ever being washed up, fill it with water and bring to the boil') appeared in Anna Haycraft and Caroline Blackwood's inspirational book, *Darling, You Shouldn't Have Gone to So Much Trouble*.

If you are intent on making soup, rather than opening up a tin or a fancy carton, it helps to have a basic jumping-off point: a recipe which enables you to concoct a humdinger of a dinner-party soup or just use up whatever happens to be lurking at the back of the fridge. As anyone with pretensions to cooking will tell you, the stock is what counts: if you make a soup with chicken stock boiled up from the carcass of the Sunday roast, it'll taste much better than if you just simmer a lot of disparate ingredients in a pan of water.

Fergus Henderson describes what goes into a stock, without actually providing a recipe, in *Nose to Tail Eating*: bones, giblets or shells, an onion (halved but unpeeled), garlic (one bulb, again unpeeled and chopped in half), a carrot, a leek maybe, some herbs, maybe a few peppercorns and a litre or two of water. Simmer away on a low heat in a lidded pan for two to three hours. Once it's done, strain out the bits and pieces and return the soup to the pan for when you need it. You can keep a pan of stock on the back of the stove for days, boiling it up now and again to prevent it going off.

Once you've got the stock, you need a recipe. John Tovey's basic vegetable soup recipe, from *A Feast of Vegetables*, can be adapted to suit pretty much any soup you care to mention. As he says (in jovial italics), 'This is a basic recipe for *every single vegetable soup mentioned in this book*', but you can use it as a blueprint for meat-based soups as well. If you have any leftovers, you can freeze them in an ice-cube tray and when the cubes become solid, store in a plastic bag in the freezer – the homemade equivalent of cup-a-soup.

Basic soup

(from *Feast of Vegetables* by John Tovey)

Enough for 12 small or 6 large portions

> *100 g (4 oz) butter*
> *225 g (8 oz) onions, finely chopped*
> *900 g (2 lb) prepared vegetables (or whatever you*
> *happen to be using, chopped to similar sizes)*
> *150 ml (¼ pint) cooking sherry (optional but*
> *preferable) or water*
> *850 ml–1 litre (1½–2 pints) stock*

In a large saucepan, melt the butter. Add the onions and cook until golden. Then add the vegetables and any flavourings, herbs, etc. that you are using. Pour in the sherry or water. Cover the pan and simmer over a low heat for 35–40 minutes until the vegetables are soft enough to be liquidised. (Keep an eye on the pan to make sure nothing sticks or burns; add a little water if it does.) Add the stock and liquidise the soup. If you don't like smooth soup, don't liquidise. Return the soup to the pan and reheat, adding seasoning when needed.

Curry

Making a curry is like gardening – you only do it when you've got your own kitchen. Otherwise it's a takeaway, or a cheap meal out, or something your mother used to make on Monday nights from leftover roast lamb with little side-dishes of sliced banana, desiccated coconut and raisins. If you're going to make it yourself, you need a basic recipe and a well-stocked spice cupboard. The best recipe I've found – one which uses not too frightening quantities of spices in manageable combinations – is in Camellia Panjabi's *50 Great Indian Curries.* Panjabi, who in her youth attended Queen

Mary's school, Bombay, but is now the driving force behind Veeraswamy's, Chutney Mary and Amaya in London, has made it her life's work to track down obscure curries, one of which was the mutton dish she was given at Queen Mary's: 'I searched for years for the exact replica of the mutton curry. Once, in the mid-Sixties, I found it accidentally on the buffet table of the West End Hotel in Bangalore.'

The mutton curry duly appears in *50 Great Indian Curries,* but it's the Simple Homestyle Curry you want to go for. Use it with chicken, lamb, fish or vegetables – it will transform the most tragic leftovers into a swish dinner, filling your kitchen with that authentic curry aroma as an additional treat. It is a hundred times better than anything you'll get out of a jar or a packet. Panjabi is obsessive about times of cooking, but I've found that instinct works just as well as clock-watching. Use her timings as guidelines and be relaxed about the spices – this curry works whether you have everything or not. A vital tip: get all the ingredients for the sauce out of the cupboard before you start and put them away as you use them; this saves a lot of swearing and shouting.

Simple homestyle chicken curry

(from *50 Great Curries of India* by Camellia Panjabi)

Serves 2

> 4 tablespoons oil
> 1 large onion, finely chopped
> 2 cloves of garlic, chopped ¼ inch square
> piece of fresh ginger, chopped
> ½ teaspoon coriander powder
> a pinch of turmeric powder
> ½ teaspoon cumin powder
> ½ teaspoon garam masala powder
> 1 teaspoon paprika
> 2 tomatoes, chopped
> salt
> chopped coriander leaves to garnish

To make the sauce: heat the oil in a heavy pan. Add the onion and sauté over a medium heat for about 20–25 minutes, or until deep brown. Add the garlic and ginger and fry for 1 minute. Add the coriander powder and stir for a further full minute. Then add the turmeric, cumin, garam masala and paprika and sauté for 30 seconds. Add 1 cup water and cook for 10 minutes. Put in the

tomatoes, stir well and cook for a further 5 minutes.
Add salt to taste.

Add chicken [or lamb, fish or vegetables] and 1½ cups
of water [adjust the water to suit the ingredients you are
adding – more for lamb, slightly less for fish]. Cook for
20–25 minutes until the chicken etc. is cooked through.
Sprinkle with coriander leaves just before serving.
Serve with rice, or pitta bread.

Ms Panjabi is the modern face of curry making. In 1948,
you might have had to make do with the recipe devised
by Mr Wilson Midgley, though it is by no means the worst
you could have found: 'Simple Curry. One small tin of
soup (vegetable or scotch broth), 1 tablespoon flour
(or cornflour), 1 tablespoon curry powder, left-over cold

meat. Empty the tin of soup into a pan and stir in the flour and curry powder. Stir well and bring slowly to the boil. When the mixture has boiled, put in your pieces of cold meat and keep it hot for three or four minutes, but do not let it boil again or it will toughen the meat.'

This recipe appears in Midgley's *Cookery For Men Only,* a wildly eccentric tome devoted to encouraging men to start cooking. An ex-Boy Scout, he is baffled by the modern chap's inability to see cooking as a viable evening's entertainment and sets about their re-education with evangelical fervour although, as the Index makes clear, Midgley himself has a rather troubled relationship with food. 'Frying' (subtitled 'Indigestion') is divided into 'Deep fat', 'Double', 'Shallow' and 'Wartime'. 'Drinks, stimulating' are not alcoholic beverages but 'a very strong solution of any of the commercial meat extracts in hot milk', a beverage apparently much enjoyed by Midgley and his wife after hiking for 25 miles having 'missed the train at a little junction station' (somehow you just know it was Midgley's fault).

In the helpful section entitled 'Washing up, hints on...' you discover that one method is to 'let everything pile up in the sink until your first woman relative comes home'. It would have been interesting to have heard Mrs Midgley's views on her husband's domestic arrangements, but she remains a silent, though potent, presence throughout.

Risotto

The act of cooking rice in a pot of broth had been around for centuries but it wasn't until the 19th century that the modern method of frying the grains of rice before adding the stock was adopted. Coincidentally, the 19th century was also the time when rice lost its peasant associations and became widely eaten by the rich.

As every connoisseur will tell you, the three secrets of a good risotto are the type of rice used, the time taken to cook it and the stock you cook it in. As Valentina Harris, who has made it her life's work to trace the history and provenance of risotto, says, 'If you have a good stock with plenty of flavour, it is virtually impossible to make a bad, tasteless risotto.'

The other key factor in making risotto is to go slowly – slow cooking and constant stirring. Arborio rice is suitable for all risotto, but carnaroli is excellent – the high starch content allows the grain to keep its shape and texture. You can also use Padano, Maratelli and Vialone Nano, which has a large rounded grain and makes an extra-creamy smooth risotto.

The most famous risotto of all is risotto alla Milanese. One of the first sightings of this startling dish appears in Breughel's famous painting *The Peasant Wedding* (1568). The inclusion of saffron and its resultant golden colour meant that this risotto was often associated with weddings. According to Aldo Buzzi, in his eccentric book *The Perfect Egg and Other Secrets,* the perfect way to eat a risotto alla Milanese is with pickled onions. 'Here's how', he explains: 'With your spoon, spread the risotto out well on the plate, scatter round the edge of the risotto, but without invading the edge of the plate itself, which must remain spotless, a few small Como onions pickled in red wine vinegar – and cut into four – and sprinkle the risotto with a few drops of the onion-steeped vinegar.'

Other risottos are harder to come by. I once spent a miraculous ten days in Venice searching for risi e bisi, which (I'd read somewhere) was the only type of risotto the Venetians consumed. I came across it just once, in a canal-side restaurant, and it was a deep disappointment.

Valentina Harris's recipe in *Risotto Risotto* is exactly the kind of creamy, flavoursome concoction I was hoping for. Done in the old way, without frying the grains, it is more like a very thick soup than a risotto.

Risi e bisi

(from *Risotto Risotto* by Valentina Harris)

Serves 4

> 1 kg (2½ lb) young fresh peas
>   or 500 g (1 lb 2 oz) frozen petits pois
> ½ onion, finely chopped
> 50 g (2 oz) pancetta, chopped
> 50 g (2 oz) unsalted butter
> 3 tablespoons extra virgin olive oil
> 25 g (1 oz) chopped fresh parsley
> 1.5 litres (2½ pints) beef, veal or chicken stock,
>   kept simmering
> 300 g (11 oz) risotto rice,
>   preferably Vialone Nano Gigante
> sea salt and ground black pepper
> 50 g (2 oz) Parmesan cheese, freshly grated,
>   and some extra for serving

Shell the fresh peas and rinse in cold water. Fry the onions and pancetta in the oil and butter in a heavy-based pan for about 10 minutes. Stir in the parsley and fry gently for a further 4 minutes. Then add the peas and stir thoroughly. Add just enough hot stock barely to cover the ingredients, then simmer very gently until the peas are almost tender – about 15 minutes for fresh, or 5 minutes for frozen. Add the rice, stir and add more stock. Season and stir, waiting patiently for the grains to absorb the stock before you add more. After about 20 minutes, when the rice is soft and tender, remove from the heat, stir in the cheese and leave to rest for 3 minutes before turning on to a warmed platter to serve. Serve with more grated Parmesan.

Gravy

*'There is no passion in human nature, as the passion
for gravy among commercial gentlemen. It's nothing to
say a joint won't yield – a whole   animal wouldn't yield –
the amount of gravy they expect each day at dinner'* –
Mrs Todger in *Martin Chuzzlewit*

You can't have a roast without gravy. I don't think I've
ever actually followed a recipe for gravy, which may
explain the hit and miss nature of the results. Gravy
depends to a large extent on what you put in it but it
is contrary in character – if I try very hard to make it
perfectly, it'll turn out a disaster. If I sneak up on it on
the sly as it were, it'll be brilliant. Here's what you do.

Remove the roast from the pan and skim as much of the
fat from the pan as possible. Put the pan on a medium
heat and sprinkle over a tiny amount of flour (gravy
freaks will rise up as one and yell 'don't put in any flour',
but I find it helps to soak up excess fat and gives a bit
of body) and when that's bubbling and browning, pour in
a good measure of red wine. Stir frequently, scraping up
all the leftover bits and pieces which will give the gravy
flavour. Now add stock, drained vegetable water or just
water, season with salt and pepper and carry on stirring

and adding liquid as necessary, depending on how thick
you like gravy. It should by now be a gorgeous brown
and bubbling liquid. Put a gravy dish in the oven to
warm and when you're ready, pour in the gravy –
it should be smoking hot – and serve.

In *The River Cottage Meat Book,* Hugh Fearnley-
Whittingstall includes notes on a 'posh gravy' – 500 ml
clear game stock, ideally made from pigeon bones;
about $1/4$ bottle of red wine; salt. Ensure that the stock
is quite clear. If in doubt, warm it through and strain
through a piece of muslin. Add the wine and boil hard
to reduce it to an intensely flavoured sauce with a light,
syrupy consistency. Season with salt only at the end.
I would never find a piece of muslin to do this –
you can probably get away without.

Eggs

'Excepting meat, nothing furnishes a greater variety
in the kitchen than eggs' – The French Family Cook,
a Complete System of French Cookery Adapted to the
Tables not only of the Opulent, but of Persons of
Moderate Fortune and Condition, 1793

'Her breakfast was usually a boiled egg, served in
magnificent style. She used a gold egg-cup and a gold
spoon, and two of her Indian servants, in scarlet and
gold uniforms, stood behind her chair in case she
wanted anything' – Queen Victoria's breakfast

'Never, never, no matter how hungry you are, eat
a tulip-bulb omelette' – Theodora Fitzgibbon, 1982

Scrambled eggs

There are two ways to go with an egg. You can either do it the Delia way, prosaically and as a last-ditch attempt to get your children to eat old-fashioned fast food, or you can turn the business of cooking eggs into a romantic late-night or breakfast extravaganza for two. In her wildly eccentric book, *The Eating-in-Bed Cookbook*, Barbara Ninde Byfield advocates Golden Eggs – the yolks of hard-boiled eggs mixed with caviar stuffed back into the whites and topped with sour cream and lemon juice – as the perfect thing for two people to eat in bed ('consume with a glass of champagne') but for a real touch of romantic indulgence you need Escoffier's recipe, which depends upon keeping the eggs 'soft and creamy' and cooking them very slowly with a lot of butter (one ounce for every six eggs) with cream and extra butter added at the end. Published in 1909, it's reputed to be the dish eaten by Princess Diana and Dodi Al-Fayed on their last, fateful night in Paris.

Escoffier learned to cook eggs while catering for soldiers during the Franco-Prussian War. Limited supplies of anything but eggs meant that by the end of the war he had discovered more than 300 ways of cooking them. His favourite was one of the simplest: scrambled.

Auguste Escoffier (1846–1935) whose philosophy he
summed up with the words 'Faites simple' was one
of the first chefs to gain celebrity status for something
other than his cooking (he was nabbed for fiddling the
books at the Savoy). Later he moved to the Ritz where
he emphasised his celebrity status by inventing dishes
for the famous. One of his concoctions was Peach
Melba, created for Dame Nelly Melba the opera singer.
Another was inspired by a disastrous American
expedition to the Arctic during which the explorers' ship,
Jeanette, was broken up by the ice. Escoffier was much
taken with this gruesome story and created Supremes
de Volaille Jeanette – a cold dish of poached scallops
of chicken breast decorated with tarragon and laid on
layers of foie gras mousse and chicken jelly, placed
in a dish that was 'imprisoned' in a sculpted block
of ice. It was first served at the Savoy to 300 people,
though the details of death, starvation and scurvy
presumably went unrelated at the time.

Scrambled eggs the Escoffier way

(from *How to Cook A Wolf* by M. F. K. Fisher)

> *8 good fresh eggs*
> *¹/₂ pint of rich cream – or more*
> *salt and freshly ground black pepper*
> *grated cheese, herbs, what-not, if desired*

Break the eggs gently into a cold iron skillet. Pour the cream in and stir quietly until the whole is blended but no more. Never beat or whip. Heat very slowly, stirring from the middle bottom in large curds, as seldom as possible. Never let bubble. Add seasoning at the last stir or two. This takes half an hour, it cannot be hurried. Serve on toast when it is barely firm. If herbs or cheese or mushrooms (or chicken livers and so forth) are added it should be when the eggs are half done.

It's best to remove scrambled eggs from the heat just before the point of perfection as they will continue to cook in the pan. Eat them with hot toast (don't forget to butter the toast first; you don't want to be fiddling around with butter dishes as your eggs congeal in the pan) and plenty of freshly ground black pepper.

The addition of a little parsley won't go amiss, some chopped-up smoked salmon or a grating of black truffle if you have it, but the sublime mix of hot eggs, butter, cream and toast really needs no gussying up.

Omelettes

'Let us have a dinner party all to ourselves! May I ask you to bring up some herbs from the farm garden to make a savoury omelette? Sage and thyme, mint and two onions, and some parsley' – Beatrix Potter, *Jemima Puddleduck*

Although you can trace its history back to the ancient Persians (kookoo, or kuku, is a Persian dish involving a generous amount of chopped herbs stirred into beaten eggs, fried until firm and cut into wedges for serving), the omelette is probably better known today for its starring role in the disastrous dinner party scene in *Bridget Jones's Diary.* Bridget is not the only person whose romantic life has been saved by an omelette. Jilly Cooper's characters can knock them up at the drop of a hat and in *Madam, Will You Walk,* Mary Stewart's now-dated romantic thriller set in post-war France, the heroine stops in mid-car chase to consume the perfect omelette at a roadside café, thus allowing the right man to catch up with her.

An omelette from Georges Sand's cookbook ('Should it not therefore be called Omelette Aurore?' wondered Alice B. Toklas) contains candied fruit, marrons glacés and curaçao, and was sprinkled with six powdered macaroons. In 1978, Monique van Vooren, Fulbright scholar, chanteuse, television star and Belgian junior ice-skating champion, produced *The Happy Cooker,* in which various starry characters named their perfect recipes. Gore Vidal revealed that his recipe, Gored Beluga – 'The extent of my cooking' – includes one jar of Beluga caviar shared with 'someone you adore at that particular moment' washed down with Polish vodka. Ms van Vooren's was a truffle omelette (1 oz black truffle, 4 eggs) which 'makes the perfect last-minute meal for the unexpected guest'. Exactly the right kind of thing for a woman whose travels around the world allowed her to make astonishing throwaway claims about foreign food. 'Middle Eastern food,' she remarks, 'will forever remind me of J. Paul Getty's palace in Marrakesh', and when she thinks of India ('where I was rekindling my mystic fires'), she thinks of 'my former butler'. In England she dines at the Savoy, 'seated between Nureyev and Princess Margaret. The company

was, of course, quite scintillating', though the thing
that remains in her mind that evening was 'the pudding'.
Which pudding, she fails to specify.

But, *retournons à nos oeufs.* In this country, the first
recorded omelette made its appearance in 1611 when it
was defined in Cotgrave's Dictionary as 'Haumelotte; f.
An Omelet or pancake of egges'. According to Alan
Davidson in his *Penguin Companion to Food,* it's more
likely that omelettes have been around from early
medieval times, since 'The concept of frying beaten eggs
in butter in a pan is as simple as it is brilliant.' In this
context, the French omelette – light, fluffy with a runny
interior – is 'a diversion from the mainstream', but this
is the one that springs to mind whenever anyone utters
the magic words, 'Fancy an omelette then?' As Raymond
Oliver, proprietor of Colette's favourite restaurant in
Paris, Au Grand Vefour, once noted: 'A work of art is
always an adventure; the omelette does not escape
this rule.'

But like steak, and boiled eggs, omelettes are trickier to
get right than you'd imagine. Their charm resides in their
simplicity, but the ingredients must be at their best.
Fresh eggs, good butter and a decent pan are obligatory.
Herbs are optional: Paul Bocuse's Omelette aux Fines

Herbes (in *The Cuisine of Paul Bocuse*) recommends two eggs per person, half an ounce of butter for every two eggs, one teaspoon of chopped fresh parsley and another of chopped chives.

The basic recipe appears in *The Accomplisht Cook,* Robert May's 1660 translation of a French original. It goes: 'Omelette. Break 6, 8, 10 eggs more or less, beat them together in a dish and put salt to them; then put some butter a melting in a frying pan and fry it more or less, according to your discretion, only on one side or bottom.'

This is quite a restrained recipe for May, who was chef to Queen Elizabeth I. He learnt most of his

cooking in France and practised the results during royal
festivals and spectacular banquets. His set-piece was
a pyrotechnic affair involving pies shaped like castles,
stuffed with live frogs and birds, and set alight by trains
of gunpowder which exploded, letting 'out skip some
frogs, which make the Ladies skip and shreek. Next
after the other, whence come out the Birds, who by
a natural instinct flying at the light, will put out the
Candles. So what with the flying Birds and skipping
Frogs, the one above, the other beneath, will cause
much delight and pleasure to the whole company.'

May also devised a 'Good and Diverse salad' for
his royal employer made with pomegranates, figs,
nuts, samphire, purslane, almonds, and quails' eggs,
decorated with rosemary sprigs and lemon halves, which
is often served up during Elizabethan banquet scenes
in films. Faddy actresses can almost certainly be
persuaded to eat food involving leaves and nuts. May's
other triumph was, like a precursor of Mr Kipling, an
'Extraordinary Good Cake' (his name for it), involving
a bushel of the best flour you can get, three pounds
of butter, 14 pounds of currants, three quarts of thick
cream, two pounds of sugar, three pints of ale – and
'a little rosewater'.

Omelette Arnold Bennett

(Rose Prince's version of the Savoy original,
via Marcus Wareing, from *The Daily Telegraph*)

One of the most famous omelette recipes, it was made
for the writer when he stayed some months at the
Savoy Hotel in London in 1929. The omelette has
been on the menu at the Savoy ever since.

Makes 2 omelettes

> *180 g (6 oz) Finnan haddock*
> *150 ml (5 fl oz) whole milk*
> *6 eggs, beaten*
> *1–2 tablespoons butter*

For the Hollandaise:
> *2 tablespoons white wine*
> *1 shallot*
> *1 bay leaf*
> *3 white peppercorns*
> *2 large egg yolks*
> *120 g (4 oz) butter*
> *a squeeze of lemon juice*

To finish:
> *1–2 tablespoons whipped double cream*
> *2 teaspoons grated fresh Parmesan*

Put the haddock in a pan with the milk and 3 tablespoons of water and poach until the haddock is cooked.
Remove from the heat, cool and flake the fish. Put the
wine, shallot, bay leaf and peppercorns in a pan.
Bring to the boil and cook until the wine has reduced
by a third. Strain.

To make the Hollandaise: Beat the egg yolks, then whisk
in the reduced wine. Melt the butter and slowly beat into
the egg yolks, a little at a time. Beat in the lemon juice
and season and set aside in a warm place.

Preheat the grill. Combine the cream with the
Hollandaise and half the haddock. Melt the
3 tablespoons of butter in an omelette pan, pour
in half of the beaten egg, scatter over about a half
of the remaining haddock and cook until just set.
Spoon over a half of the cream/Hollandaise mix,
sprinkle over a teaspoon of cheese and grill for a
moment until lightly burnished. Season with salt and
black pepper and serve. And repeat for the second one.

Eggs Benedict

A friend of mine, Alison Gough, has a birthday brunch
each year during which she makes, and hands out,

quantities of Eggs Benedict to the assembled guests. The brunch occurs just before Christmas, and I look forward to it all through the following year. They're without doubt the best Eggs Benedict you'll taste, so I was surprised to find out from Alison that they're actually the assembled products of two supermarkets. (Alison does admit that, when cooking for two, she makes her own Hollandaise sauce.)

Cheat's Eggs Benedict

Serves 6

6 muffins (available in a pack from Waitrose)
3 cartons of Hollandaise sauce (from
  Marks & Spencer)
6 eggs
12 rashers of bacon

Poach the eggs. Grill or fry the bacon. Split and toast the muffins. Heat the sauce in a pan and then assemble the results. Muffin base, bacon, egg, sauce and the muffin top. Serve with Buck's Fizz or strong coffee.

Soufflés

One of the best soufflés I ever tasted was at Rules Restaurant in Covent Garden, London. It was a Stilton and walnut soufflé, rich and subtle to the taste, made by a chef who has since left the restaurant. I have yearned to make it ever since, but can't bring myself to risk what would be an undoubted travesty of the original. That's the way with soufflés; they instil terror in the heart of the amateur cook, and envy in the hearts of your guests if they work. The silly thing is, *they're not that difficult* – at least if you use the foolproof recipe in *Leiths Techniques Bible.* Don't bother with the breadcrumbs, and don't be tempted to check that the soufflés are done until at least eight minutes after they went into the oven.

Cheese soufflé

(from *Leiths Techniques Bible* by Susan Spaull and Lucinda Bruce-Gardyne)

Serves 4

> *40 g (1½ oz) butter, plus extra melted
>   butter for greasing*
> *2 tablespoons dried white breadcrumbs
>   for coating*
> *30 g (1 oz) plain flour*

¹/₂ teaspoon dry English mustard

a pinch of cayenne pepper

290 ml (¹/₂ pint) milk

85 g (3 oz) strong Cheddar or Gruyère cheese,
    finely grated

4 eggs, separated

salt and freshly ground pepper

Preheat the oven to 200°C/400°F/gas mark 6. Place a baking sheet in the oven. Lightly butter 4 ramekins and coat with the breadcrumbs.

Melt the butter in a small saucepan, remove the pan from the heat and stir in the flour, mustard and cayenne. Return the pan to a medium heat and cook, stirring, until the mixture bubbles. Remove from the heat. Gradually stir in the milk to make a smooth sauce, return to the heat and bring to the boil, stirring. Allow to boil for 2 minutes. The mixture will be very thick and will leave the sides of the pan. Remove from the heat. Stir in the cheese and egg yolks. Taste for seasoning. The mixture should be very well seasoned because the flavour will be diluted by the addition of the egg whites.

Whisk the egg whites until just stiff. Mix a spoonful of the whites into the cheese mixture to loosen it. Using a large metal spoon, fold in the remaining whites. Fill the ramekins three-quarters full. Place on the heated baking sheet. Turn the oven up to 225°C/425°F/gas mark 7 and bake for 8–10 minutes until the soufflés are well risen with only a slight wobble in the centre. Serve immediately.

Vegetables

'My hearse will be followed not by mourning coaches, but by herds of oxen, sheep, swine, flocks of poultry and a small travelling aquarium of live fish, all wearing white scarves in honour of the man who perished rather than eat his fellow creatures' – the vegetarian George Bernard Shaw

'The cheapest and most disagreeable guest who ever gloomed my hearth or entered my portals was a [total abstainer and vegetarian], and she was infinitely more difficult to deal with than the most fastidious gourmand I ever knew' – The Modern Housewife, 1883

Rose Elliott is the woman to consult if you are keen to embark on a serious vegetarian diet. She has spent a lifetime – from the age of 16, at least, when she began cooking for her psychic aunt's mission – devising interesting ways of cooking vegetables. I prefer vegetables to accompany meat, so although all the following make perfectly good meals in their own right, they can all be used as side dishes to a main meal.

Cauliflower cheese

Cauliflower cheese is the kind of retro dish that is so far out of fashion that it'll shortly be appearing on expensive restaurant menus. Until that happens, and if you can smuggle it on to the table past the beady eyes of your 21st-century children, it makes a stunningly good, cheap and simple supper. Sophie Grigson makes a rather fancy version in *Country Kitchen* with anchovy fillets, crème fraîche and breadcrumbs, but I think that it pays to be a bit of a purist when cooking this particular dish. Use really strong cheese (preferably Cheddar, but Gruyère is an option) for instance, and dispose of the green bits of cauliflower.

The recipe that retains the requisite simplicity and yet elevates it to haute cuisine status belongs to Constance Spry, the subtly subversive flower-arranger who nearly brought down the Design Museum last year and whose cookery school, founded after the Second World War, formed the foundation stone for the kind of basic Anglo-French recipes which are the backbone of a decent English kitchen. Assume that the reconstruction of the cauliflower is a florist's particular peccadillo. It'll taste just as good if left in bits.

Spry's cauliflower au gratin

(from *Constance Spry Cookery Book* by Constance Spry)

> 1 x 2-lb cauliflower
> 1¼ oz butter
> 1¼ oz flour (scant)
> ½ pint of milk
> salt, pepper, nutmeg
> 1½ oz Gruyère cheese
> 1½ oz Parmesan cheese
> 2 large tablespoons fresh white breadcrumbs
> 1½ oz butter

Preheat the oven to 180°C/350°F/gas mark 4. Cook the cauliflower in the French way (i.e. break into florets and boil in salted water for 15 minutes, drain immediately they are tender, and reshape into a cauliflower shape in a flameproof serving dish). Melt the butter in a saucepan and stir in the flour until smooth. Add the milk a little at a time to start with, put salt, pepper and nutmeg into the saucepan and stir till boiling. Leave to simmer for 4–5 minutes. Meanwhile, grate the cheese and add 2 spoonfuls of each kind to the crumbs. Add the remainder of the cheese to the sauce and beat until perfectly mixed and very creamy. Spoon the sauce over the cauliflower florets and sprinkle over the crumb mixture and dot with butter. Brown in a hot oven for 8–10 minutes.

Broad beans

They are the origin of the term, beanfeast: when George III went to view the progress of the building of Woolwich Arsenal, he ate with the workmen who were having beans and bacon – and he liked it so much, he instituted an annual beanfeast. They were also a favourite of Alexander Dumas, who ate them with wine and sugar. Broad beans were many centuries later given a starring role in *The Silence of the Lambs* as the

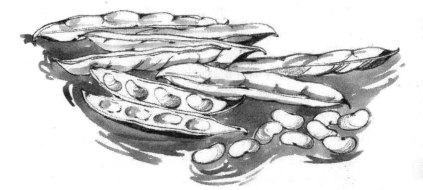

cannibal's vegetable of choice ('I ate his liver with some fava beans and a big Amarone'). Beans and bacon is an old English cottage dish (cook a piece of gammon in red wine, sugar, cloves and enough water to cover. Twenty minutes before you think it's ready, cook the shelled beans in boiling water. Pile everything on a plate and serve with parsley sauce), which was also popular as a summer side dish in great houses.

Bean fanatics will tell you to blanch and peel the broad beans before you cook them, and it's indisputable that this heaves them on to a different culinary level altogether. Hey, life's just too short. In Nigel Slater's description of Broad Beans with Ham, in *Real Fast Food* (which requires nothing but bacon, beans, olive oil and black pepper), he recommends peeling the beans but 'only if you have some time on your hands'. Eat with a bottle of beer.

If you want a slightly more sophisticated version, you need Anna del Conte's *Concise Gastronomy of Italy*, containing her recipe for Fave col Guanciale (guanciale is the cured jowl of a pig – if you can't get hold of one, use pancetta).

Fave col guanciale

(from *Concise Gastronomy of Italy* by Anna del Conte)

Serves 4

> 200 g (7 oz) pancetta, cut into cubes
> 1 small onion, chopped
> 4 tablespoons extra virgin olive oil
> 2 kg (4½ lb) fresh young broad beans
>   (fava), shelled
> about 150 ml (5 fl oz) vegetable stock or water
> salt and pepper

Fry the pancetta with the onion in the olive oil for a good 10 minutes, stirring frequently. Add the beans and coat them in the fat for 2–3 minutes and then add 100 ml (3½ fl oz) of the stock or water. Cover and cook over a low heat until the beans are tender, but still whole, about 10 minutes. You may need to add a little more of the stock during cooking.

In Italy, broad beans are eaten young and raw, served in their pods with a slice of pecorino cheese, at the end of a meal. Southern Italian cooking has many recipes for broad beans which are used fresh in the spring and dried all year round. One of the oldest of these recipes,

a purée of broad beans, originated in Egypt and consists
of the puréed beans dressed with olive oil and served,
in Sicily at least, with wild fennel, chicory or turnip tops.
You can make a version of this by frying onion, garlic
and parsley in oil, adding a couple of handfuls of broad
beans and a little water. When the beans are tender,
purée them with a hand-held mixer and stir into a bowl
of pasta.

Bubble and squeak

Nigel Slater's version of bubble and squeak, composed
of Sunday lunch leftovers – chopped cabbage, the
remains of the beef fried up in a pan with a glass of
red wine – has proved an invaluable staple on Monday
evenings. It's a recipe that harks back to the 19th
century, when Dr Kitchiner in *The Cook's Oracle* (1817)
gave a recipe for cold roast beef and green cabbage
('When midst the frying pan in accents savage/The beef,
so surly, quarrels with the cabbage'). This recipe is the
same as that given in the 1806 edition of *A New System
of Domestic Cookery* by Mrs Rundell. In 1861 Mrs
Beeton added an onion, but almost all the later recipes
omit the onion and add potato. Although it seems faintly
ridiculous to include a recipe for bubble and squeak –

surely the epitome of the shove-everything-you've-got-into-the-pan school of cooking – Dr Kitchiner's version, as supplied by Elisabeth Ayrton in *The Cookery of England,* is probably one of the most authentic you could have. (Ayrton has reinstated the controversial onion – include it or not as you will.)

I was recently informed by an Irish friend whose mother used to cook bubble and squeak for him, that leftover roast potatoes will do just as well, if not better, than mashed. He (or his mother) also thinks that leftover sprouts can be substituted for the cabbage though 'obviously, cabbage is best'. He is against the onion. Delia had a rather fashionable version in her last book, *Delia's Kitchen Garden* – Bubble and Squeak Rosti: grated cooked potato, cabbage or spring greens and cheese, shaped into rounds and baked in the oven.

Bubble and squeak

(from *The Cookery of England* by Elisabeth Ayrton)

Serves 4

> *16 slices of lean cold roast beef*
> *butter or olive oil*

1 green cabbage, finely chopped
1 onion, chopped
500 g (1 lb) cooked mashed potato

Lightly dust the beef with pepper and brown in a frying
pan with a little butter or oil. Remove and keep warm.
Boil the cabbage in a little water until tender. Drain well.
Fry the onion in the butter in which the beef was fried,
adding more oil if necessary. When soft, add the
cabbage and potato and cook until it forms a cake.
Turn the cake once, fry a little more, and then serve on
a flat dish with the beef around it and some good gravy.

Lentil sauce

Shaun Hill served up this lentil sauce with scallops
at the Merchant House in Ludlow. Hill has reached
further heights of culinary fame, but his recipe is as
good as ever. It can also be used with chicken. I have
substituted cardamom seeds for ground cardamom,
learning by experiment that, although deseeding
cardamom pods is a pain in the neck, it is definitely
worth taking the trouble or finding a smallish child
to take the trouble for you. Here's the recipe minus
the scallops.

Lentil and coriander sauce

(from *How to Cook Better* by Shaun Hill)

Serves 4

50 g brown lentils

a little groundnut or sunflower oil

$\frac{1}{2}$ onion, finely chopped

1 tablespoon chopped red pepper

1 tablespoon chopped fresh ginger

1 large clove garlic, chopped

$\frac{1}{2}$ teaspoon ground cardamom

$\frac{1}{2}$ teaspoon ground coriander

$\frac{1}{2}$ teaspoon ground cinnamon

$\frac{1}{2}$ teaspoon ground cumin

300 ml chicken stock or water

25 g unsalted butter

1 teaspoon crème fraîche

1 tablespoon fresh coriander leaves,
    roughly chopped

1 tablespoon snipped fresh chives

1 tablespoon lemon juice

salt and pepper

Put the lentils in tepid water and soak for 2 hours.
Simmer for around 10 minutes, or until cooked through.

Heat a little sunflower or groundnut oil to a high
temperature. Fry the onion, red pepper, ginger and
garlic until they start to caramelise, then add the spices
and half the cooked lentils, then strain the stock on
to the spiced lentils. Bring to the boil and simmer for
5 minutes. Purée the lentil mixture in a liquidiser,
then reheat with butter, crème fraîche, coriander leaves,
chives and lemon juice. Season with salt and pepper,
then add the remaining cooked lentils. Spoon this
sauce on to warmed plates.

Creamed leek with orange

This is one in a series of Sophie Grigson's *Sunday Times*
Cookery Cards, published in the 90s, which came free
with the paper. As a way of gussying up leeks it is
unbeatable and goes extremely well with roast lamb.

Creamed leek with orange

(from *Sunday Times* Cookery Card by Sophie Grigson)

Serves 4-6

> *5 large leeks trimmed, cut into 4-cm*
> *(1½-inch) lengths and shredded finely*
> *45 g (1½ oz) butter*
> *juice of 1 orange*
> *salt and pepper*
> *45 g (1½ oz) flour*
> *300 ml (½ pint) milk*
> *finely grated zest of 1 orange*
> *squeeze of lemon juice*

Melt the butter in a wide frying pan and add the leeks.
Stir to mix and then add the orange juice and a little salt
and pepper. Cover and simmer gently for 5–10 minutes
until virtually all the liquid has evaporated. Sprinkle
with flour and stir for 1 minute. Gradually add the milk,
stirring, then the orange zest. Bring up to a simmer
and cook for 3–5 minutes until thick and creamy.
Add more milk if necessary. Season with salt and
pepper and stir in a dash of lemon juice.

Peas with lettuce

'Wednesday. A big bowl of very small fresh peas cooked with little shreds of lettuce but without the little onions usually associated with the à la française manner of cooking them. The result was very creamy and good. I doubt if I shall ever again put onions with my peas' –
Elizabeth David, *An Omelette and a Glass of Wine*

Once you've eaten stewed peas, you can't imagine why you ever mess around with the frozen variety – how did it happen that fresh peas in pods in supermarkets are now as rare as hens' teeth? Stewed fresh peas with cream and butter used to be part of our national repertoire, as evinced by Hannah Glasse in *Art of Cookery,* subtly different from the French version with lettuce, but if you like the idea, Hannah's is the one to go for. It's quick, easy and unfussy.

For six people, 'Take a quart [1½ lb] of fine green peas, put them in a stewpan with a piece of butter as big as an egg, rolled in a little flour, season them with salt and nutmeg, a bit of sugar as big as a nutmeg, a little bundle of sweet herbs, some parsley chopped fine, a quarter of a pint of boiling water. Cover them close, and let them stew very softly half an hour, then pour on a quarter of a pint of good cream. Give it one boil and serve it up for a side plate.'

Elizabeth David's recipe in *French Provincial Cooking* eschews the cream (and here she has left out the onions, though there are other versions of this recipe which don't) and takes into account the fact that you're probably going to be cooking full-grown English peas, not the baby French variety. She uses 3 lb of peas, which she cooks in a small amount of boiling water with one small lettuce heart and a lump of sugar. Cook until the peas are tender, drain and return them to the pan with a large lump of butter – 'a quarter pound is by no means too much' – and leave the peas and lettuce to stew in the butter for a few minutes.

Mushrooms

According to Alan Davidson, 'authors of mushroom books, haunted by visions of readers collapsing in agony after eating toxic species', have historically piled 'warnings and cautionary tales upon each other to such an extent that their works seem to be funerary rather than culinary.' The exception to this gloomy rule was Charles Mcilvaine who in *One Thousand American Fungi* (1902) positively spurs on the hesitant. 'Reputed to be harmful,' he will observe, 'but never did me any harm!'

Britain grew up under the shadow of the English herbalists who, almost to a man, regarded fungi with deep suspicion. *The Grete Herbal* (1526) declared that 'There be two manners of them, one manner is deedly and sleath them that eateth of them and be called tode stoles.' A hundred years later, Gerard in his Herbal was warning that 'Most of them do suffocate and strangle the eater', and in 1783 John Farley, in *The London Art of Cookery,* described them warily, yet poetically as 'treacherous gratifications. Those employed in collecting them should be extremely cautious.'

This is not how the rest of Europe views the mushroom, or Russia where children learning the alphabet see by a picture that 'g' stands for *grib* (mushroom) and sing a marching song, reminiscent in tone to 'The Grand Old Duke of York', entitled 'Panic Among the Mushrooms'. Nowadays, however, you have to be more careful with Russian mushrooms, not because of their possible poisonous nature, but because, Davidson says, 'they have undergone some crucial change, possibly caused by radiation'.

Panicking among the mushrooms is, ironically, what we've been doing in the UK for the last five hundred years or so, until rescue arrived in the form of Antonio Carluccio, the Italian mushroom maestro now relocated to Petersfield in Hampshire, where he conducts mushroom hunts in the rolling countryside of the North Downs. Carluccio's autumnal mushroom markets, held in and around London, give a vibrant taste of the mushroom markets of Italy, Poland and France.

Despite, or even because of, the scary reputation of the mushroom, one of the first things my son Max learnt to cook and can produce by himself (along with a cup of tea) was mushrooms on toast. He cuts mushrooms into quarters, melts some butter in a pan and fries the mushrooms in the butter and then adds cream, salt and pepper and dishes the lot up on toast. Delicious, especially when done for you. There are other ways to do it, though; in *Spices, Salt and Aromatics in the English Kitchen,* the omniscient Elizabeth David has a recipe for coriander mushrooms which makes the best of the firm white kind you're likely to find in a supermarket.

Coriander mushrooms

(from *Spices, Salt and Aromatics in the English Kitchen* by Elizabeth David)

Serves 3

> *170 g (6 oz) firm, white, round, fresh mushrooms*
> *1 teaspoon coriander seeds, crushed in a mortar*
> *2 tablespoons olive oil*
> *lemon juice,*
> *salt and pepper*
> *1 or 2 bay leaves*

Rinse the mushrooms, dry with a clean cloth and cut into quarters (or into eighths if they are large). Squeeze over them a little lemon juice. Warm the olive oil in a frying pan, add the crushed coriander seeds and cook for a few seconds over a low heat. Add the mushrooms and the bay leaves. Add the seasoning.

Let the mushrooms cook gently for a minute, cover the pan and leave them, on a very low heat, for another 3–5 minutes. Uncover the pan and decant the mushrooms, and the bay leaves, with all their juices into a shallow serving dish and sprinkle with fresh olive oil and lemon juice. Serve hot or cold.

Aubergines

If you are in possession of a packet of pitta bread and an aubergine, you've got lunch – pretty much. This is an easy version of an Arabic staple, Baba Kannouj, dreamed up by Mohammed Bahzad Barafi, speciality Arabic chef at Al Qasr in Dubai. It takes about five minutes to prepare once the aubergine has cooled, and produces a wonderful aroma of Middle Eastern cooking while you do it.

Baba Kannouj

(Mohammed Bahzad Barafi)

Serves 4 as a dip

> *1 kg skinless roasted aubergine (see below)*
> *100 g tomato, chopped*
> *100 g onion, chopped*

50 g red, yellow and green peppers, finely chopped
1 clove garlic, crushed
20 g mint or parsley, chopped
100 ml lemon juice
100 ml olive oil
20 g salt
50 g pomegranate seeds

Skin the aubergine by roasting it in the oven or leaving it on a hot plate, turning from time to time. Once cooled, chop the aubergine finely and mix it with the tomato, onion, peppers, and garlic if you are serving it immediately. If not, save the garlic until just before you serve. Stir in the lemon juice and salt. Add the chopped mint or parsley just before serving, garnish with olive oil and scatter on the pomegranate seeds.

Tomato sauce for pasta

Marcella Hazan's spiritual home was Venice, but with her matronly looks and her penchant for three slugs of whisky at lunchtime, she became the darling of America – the woman who introduced her host country (she now lives in Florida) to the idea that Italian food need not entirely consist of pizza and spaghetti bolognaise (which was never Italian in the first place).

But despite her reciprocated passion for the USA, Hazan never reconciled her belief in spontaneous cooking with the American desire for careful measuring. It took her five years' hard graft to translate her erratic Italian recipes into precise American. 'We did it in the Hamptons,' her long-suffering husband Victor explained, 'in a house with a swimming pool which I used only three times all the years we spent there.' Perhaps because of this, *Marcella's Italian Kitchen* (1986) was Hazan's last book, a distillation of the previous three, all of which extolled the notion of simple Italian cooking using the freshest ingredients.

One of the recipes which best embodies Hazan's philosophy is Spaghettini col Sugo di Erbe e Pomodoro Crudo (thin spaghetti with herbs and raw tomato). This is the reverse of the slow-cooked tomato sauce, a classic in itself, but it makes the most of an increasing feature of British supermarkets – 'tomatoes grown for their flavour'. Hazan notes that this sauce for spaghettini or maccheroncini 'doesn't even take one minute. The herbs and tomatoes go directly into the serving bowl where they are splashed with hot olive oil. It is in that brief second or two, while the heat is at flash point, that the fruity scent of the sizzling olive oil is fused to the fresh aromas of the five herbs and the tomato.'

Tomato sauce

(from *Marcella's Italian Kitchen* by Marcella Hazan)

Serves 4–6

> 1½ lb fresh tomatoes
> 3 tablespoons fresh basil, chopped
> 1 tablespoon chopped fresh sage
> 3 tablespoons chopped parsley
> 3 teaspoons fresh rosemary, chopped fine
> 1 tablespoon chopped fresh mint
> 1 lb spaghettini
> ⅓ cup extra virgin olive oil
> salt and black pepper

Wash the tomatoes, split in half, remove the seeds
and dice the halves into ½-inch cubes. Put the diced
tomatoes, the basil, sage, parsley, rosemary and mint
into the bowl in which you'll be tossing and serving
the pasta. Drop the spaghettini into a pot of abundant
boiling, salted water. When the pasta is nearly done,
put the olive oil into a small saucepan and turn the heat
to high. When the oil is smoking hot, pour it over the
tomatoes and herbs in the serving bowl. It should be
hot enough to sizzle as it hits the contents of the bowl.
Add salt, pepper and mix well. When the pasta is done

(barely tender but firm to the bite), drain it well and transfer immediately to the bowl, tossing it thoroughly with all the ingredients. Serve promptly.

Caesar salad

Eighty-one years old and still sound in wind and limb, Caesar salad is one of the 20th-century's more enduring recipes. It may have suffered some indignities along the way, but the basic premise of lettuce, mayonnaise, cheese and garlicky bread is still largely intact. It was invented by Caesar Cardini on 4 July 1924, in Tijuana, Mexico, when a party of visiting revellers arrived unexpectedly at the Cardini restaurant demanding

a late lunch. There was nothing in the kitchen but stale bread, old Parmesan, lettuce leaves, Worcestershire sauce and eggs. Cardini took this insalubrious collection of ingredients to the table and mixed them in front of everyone.

Julia Child recorded the event in her book *Julia Child's Kitchen:* 'Caesar rolled the big cart up to the table and tossed the Romaine in a big wooden bowl, and I wish I could say I remember his every move, but I don't. The only thing I see again clearly are the eggs. I can see him break two eggs over that Romaine and roll them in; the greens going all creamy as the eggs flowed over them.' There were no anchovies in the original, just an essence of them in the Worcestershire sauce. Adding pounded anchovies became common practice later.

Caesar salad

(Caesar Cardini, from *Julia Child's Kitchen* by Julia Child)

Serves 4–6

> *2 cloves of garlic, crushed*
> *175 ml (6 fl oz) olive oil*
> *6 tablespoons cubed white bread,*
>   *use good French-style sourdough*

leaves from 2 heads of Romaine lettuce,
or 4 baby cos, washed and chilled
2 eggs, boiled in the shell for 1 minute
juice of 2 lemons
8 drops of Worcestershire sauce
6 tablespoons freshly grated Parmesan cheese

Put the garlic in the olive oil and leave for 1 hour or more to infuse. Preheat the oven to 200°C/400°F/gas mark 6. Brush the bread with some of the oil and bake until golden. Put the leaves in a big bowl and break the eggs over them. Toss the salad slowly, then add the lemon juice, the Worcestershire sauce and seasoning. Toss the salad again. Add the cheese, toss one more time and serve.

Puddings

'Let us seriously reflect on what a pudding is composed of. It is composed of flour, that once waved in the golden grain, and drank the dews of the morning; of milk pressed from the swelling udder by the gentle hand of the beautiful milkmaid ... who, while she stroked the udder, indulged in no ambitious thoughts of wandering in palaces, formed no plans for the destruction of her fellow creatures' – James Boswell

Crumb Pudding: 'Save all the crumbs left upon the table during the week, and add to these any waste pieces of bread. Put them into a basin with two ounces of treacle mixed up with them. Soak them in enough water to make them swell. Then tie them in a cloth and boil for half an hour' – The Dictionary of Daily Wants, 1859

The best puddings are generally found in other people's houses or, as my children believe, in the ice-cream freezer at Waitrose, but if you are determined to produce dessert, the following are impressive as well as filling.

Tarte Tatin

One of the most famous fans of tarte Tatin (he ate
the original version, made by the Tatin sisters at their
restaurant in Sologne, frequently travelling the 60 miles
or so in an early motor car to do so), was the painter
Claude Monet. Cantankerous, autocratic and mostly
broke, Monet's domestic life would make rich material
for a modern day sitcom. Beset by children (at one time
he had eight or nine living in the house with him, not all
his own) and married to a woman whose ex-husband had
lost all his money investing in the Impressionists, he
always went to bed at 9.30 pm and counted it a disaster
if he were forced to stay up any later. He ate Stilton
and tripe sausages for breakfast, a habit picked up
in England and spent twenty years trying to get over
the day the cook served banana ice cream made with
kitchen salt instead of sugar. The incident became
a joke on its 21st anniversary.

He and his wife Alice grew all their own fruit and
vegetables, their 'sole culinary ambition' being the now
hugely fashionable one of serving 'beautifully prepared
dishes using whatever the kitchen garden or the farmyard
could supply'. Monet was a scavenger when it came
to recipes: apart from the Tatin tart, his bouillabaisse

was originally concocted by Paul Cezanne, and his bread rolls were devised by Jean Millet.

The point about tarte Tatin is that it's made of apples – nothing else. Never be seduced into making mango or onion Tatin – only the apple has the sweetness and acidity necessary to complement the flavour of the caramel and the buttery pastry. Monet's recipe uses 6 russet apples and half a pound of unsalted butter, and he served the tart pastry up. This version of tarte Tatin, possibly the best I've ever tasted, comes from Rowley Leigh's *No Place Like Home* and was discovered by my daughter Sophie, whose social life has often been compromised by the pleas of visitors to get back in the kitchen and make another one.

Tarte Tatin

(from *No Place Like Home* by Rowley Leigh)

> 2 lemons
> 2 kg Cox's apples
> 125 g unsalted butter, lightly softened
> 125 g caster sugar
> 200 g puff pastry

Leigh says that a really heavy pan, about 22–24 cm in diameter with straight sides is pretty well essential. Cox's are good because they have the necessary acidity to counterbalance the sugar and don't fall apart during cooking. Squeeze the juice of the lemons and put in a large bowl with a couple of tablespoons of water. Peel and halve the apples, remove the cores with a teaspoon and roll the halves in the juice. Smear the butter generously all over the base and sides of the cold pan. Sprinkle the sugar on top and give the pan a shake to ensure the sugar is evenly distributed. Drain the apples and arrange them on their sides in concentric circles, embedding them in the butter sugar mix. Pack them in as tightly as you can, then put the pan on the fiercest heat you have.

While keeping a beady eye on the pan, roll out the pastry into a disc about 2 cm wider than the rim of the pan. Leave it to rest on a sheet of greaseproof paper on a plate in the fridge. Watch the sides of the pan closely. You are looking for a good rich caramel colour to develop. Move the pan around on the heat to ensure the mixture caramelises evenly. It can take 10–20 minutes. When it is done, transfer the pan to a heatproof surface. After 5 minutes or so, when the pan has cooled a little, drop the disc of pastry on to the apples and let the edges hang over the side of the pan.

Place the pan in an oven preheated to 220°C/425°F/ gas mark 7 and bake for 15 minutes, or until the pastry is nicely risen. Remove from the oven and leave to rest for a minute.

The hard part is getting the tarte out of the tin, and for this you need strong wrists and nerves of steel. Don't attempt to do this in front of your guests – one of the advantages of this particular tarte is that it tastes OK even if it collapses completely and looks a total mess, but better not to let your fellow diners see the disaster in action.

To get the tarte out, according to Leigh, place an inverted plate, slightly bigger than the pan, over the top. With one hand firmly in place over the plate, grip the handle equally firmly with your other hand and a cloth and, with a determined turn of the wrist, flip the pan over on to the plate. Lower the plate on to a surface, pause for a moment and then lift off the pan. Behold, one hopes, a perfect golden circle of apples. If things have shifted move them back into place with a palette knife. Serve warm with double cream.

Christmas pudding

In *Spices, Salt and Aromatics in the English Kitchen*, Elizabeth David recounted how she had been 'nagged into making a Christmas pudding' thirty years earlier by her village neighbours on the island of Syros in the Cyclades. 'There were luscious local raisins, currants from Zante, almonds from the mainland, citron grown and candied on a neighbouring island, beef suet from the town butcher, Greek brandy. The eggs were new laid.' Everything – including the stoning of the raisins and the skinning of the suet – had to be done by hand. 'After two long days in the kitchen, I had some understanding of the tedious jobs the cooks and

kitchen maids of the past were obliged to perform,'
David wrote.

She had used her sister's recipe, scribbled on the back
of an envelope, and subsequently lost. The one that
was printed in *Salt and Aromatics* came from *The Ocklye
Cookery Book,* a pre-1914 family recipe book kept
by Eleanor Jenkinson, whose librarian brother was
'incidentally responsible for introducing the recipe for
crème brûlée to the kitchens of Trinity College,
Cambridge, where it became famous.'

The Ocklye pudding is a bit of a labour of love, I think.
Luckily you'll only be making it once a year, as it produces

a massive amount of pudding and you'll need most of a day to do it properly, no distractions of the child/demanding-husband type, plenty of space and a radio to listen to. Later on in the process you can gather your whole family together to help with the stirring and at that point you will feel that you are creating something pleasingly, indeed uniquely in this day and age, traditional and Christmassy. Without wishing to get too sentimental about it, it's something your children will remember into old age, much as they remember podding peas and picking brambles and other increasingly rare country pursuits. Health freaks will be interested to know that the Ocklye pudding is surprisingly good for you – it contains no sugar and you can substitute half a pint of stout for the milk. The result is fantastically chewy and flavoursome.

Plum pudding

(from *Elizabeth David's Christmas*, edited by Jill Norman)

'Two pounds and a quarter (1.1 kg) of stoned raisins, two pounds and a quarter (1.1 kg) of currants, six ounces (180 g) of finely chopped candied peel, thirteen eggs, one pint and a half (900 ml) of milk, one teacupful and a half of breadcrumbs, one pound and a half

(750 g) of flour, one pound and a half (750 g) of finely chopped suet, three wine glasses of brandy, two wine-glasses of rum.

'Mix these ingredients well together, put into buttered basins, and boil for fourteen hours. The quantity makes 2 large puddings.'

1. For mixing the pudding you need a really capacious bowl and a stout wooden spoon — and as everybody in the family is supposed to take a hand in the job, this part of it should not be very hard work. It's all done on the day before the puddings are supposed to be cooked, and the mixture is left overnight in the covered bowl, in a cool place. Some people think it a mistake to add the brandy, rum and ale until the next day, but it's easier to do all the mixing in one go. In a single night the fruit isn't going to start fermenting.

2. The ritual silver coins, ring, thimble and other pudding favours can be put into each pudding when the basins are packed – they're supposed to be wrapped in greaseproof paper, more so that they can be found than for hygienic reasons. But if there are children it's better to slip them surreptitiously on the plates when the pudding is served so that they are easily seen. The drama of inadvertently swallowed coins and charms

is something one can do without on Christmas Day.
3. The pudding will swell during cooking, so allow for
this by leaving an inch or so (2–3 cm) of space at the
top when the mixture is packed into the buttered basins.
4. Cover each pudding with buttered greaseproof paper
before tying on the cloths.

For steaming the pudding on Christmas Day: Elizabeth
David advises steaming the pudding for a good
two hours on the day, then allowing it to stand for
10 minutes before turning it out on to a plate and
pouring over warmed rum or brandy that has been
lit with a match.

Brandy butter

In 1932, *The Daily Telegraph* published a book of *Four
Hundred Prize Recipes,* one of which was a recipe for
brandy butter 'composed by Professor Hardy, member of
Sidney Sussex College, Cambridge'. This was usually
called Professor Hardy's Sauce and is the foundation of
the brandy butter now served.

Brandy butter

(from *Four Hundred Prize Recipes*)

> 125 g (¼ lb) butter
> a generous 125 g (¼ lb) finely powdered sugar
> [Prof. Hardy recommends 'rather more'
> sugar than butter, but that is really up
> to individual taste]
> grated nutmeg
> 1 tablespoon brandy
> 2 tablespoons sherry

In a bowl, beat the butter and sugar well together, until quite white and light. Then add a little grated nutmeg. Add the brandy and sherry 'slowly, by degrees, beating thoroughly all the time until mixed'. Serve very cold piled up in a glass cup or boat.

The Telegraph also published, in the same book of recipes, a version of Cumberland butter. Cream 125 g (4 oz) of warmed butter with 350 g (¾ lb) Barbados sugar (the treacly dark brown sugar found at wholefood stores); add 15 g (½ oz) grated nutmeg, a pinch of cinnamon and beat well. Then add ¾ of a wineglassful of rum and beat again. Serve in 'a small glass or china bowl, and sift caster sugar over it'.

Those wanting a modern spin on butters to accompany their Christmas pud should try the recipe devised by Angela Hartnett, Head Chef at the Connaught and one of Gordon Ramsey's protégées, which uses a fraction of the sugar and adds lemon juice at the end.

Brandy butter

(Angela Hartnett)

> 100 g (3 oz) unsalted butter
> 100 g (3 oz) caster sugar
> 2 tablespoons brandy
> 1 teaspoon lemon juice

Have your butter at room temperature. Beat it until soft and creamy. Slowly add the sugar then gradually add the brandy. Finally, stir in the lemon juice. Chill for a few hours before serving.

Bread and butter pudding

Bread and butter pudding is one of the most flexible dishes. You can make it with panettone, croissants

(even pain au chocolat) or hot cross buns as well as
bread. Tom Norrington-Davies's recipe (strictly speaking,
one devised by his friend John) is one of the best:
'There is no finer use for a slice of stale bread,' he
states. And it must be stale bread, otherwise the whole
thing turns out too soggy. I would be more profligate with
the dried fruit and throw in some currants as well – quite
a lot in fact, since I believe that you can't really make
bread and butter pudding without them.

Bread and butter pudding

(from *Just Like Mother Used to Make*
by Tom Norrington-Davies)

Serves 4

> *8 slices of stale white bread, buttered*
> *50 g (2 oz) mixed dried fruit*
> *3 eggs*
> *2 level tablespoons caster sugar*
> *2 drops of vanilla essence*
> *200 ml (7 fl oz) whole milk*
> *100 ml (3½ fl oz) double cream*
> *2 tablespoons soft brown sugar (optional)*

Preheat the oven to 180°C/350°F/gas mark 4. Cut the bread into soldiers. Arrange the bread and the fruits in a small baking dish or ovenproof bowl in layers. In a separate bowl, beat the eggs with the sugar and vanilla, then beat in the milk and cream. Pour this over the bread and sprinkle the top with brown sugar. Leave to rest in a cool place for at least an hour, then bake in the oven for 30 minutes. When it's done, allow to rest for 10 minutes before serving.

Summer pudding

Like some early precursor of the modish dietary fad, summer pudding used to be known as 'hydropathic pudding' and was served up at health resorts where pastry was forbidden. That seems almost inconceivable now, in these days of carb and wheat-free diets. Summer pudding, much sought after amongst pudding freaks, now has a whiff of decadent excess about it, though I remember from my childhood that we thought it quite horrendously boring – too much stale white bread and too little fruit. An Indian missionary, Miss E. S. Poynter, seems to have been the first to use the modern term, summer pudding, in 1904; in 1912 the name was taken up by Miss L. Sykes whose recipe was very similar to today's version.

I found one of my favourite recipes for summer pudding
in *The Food of Love,* which started out as a collection
of recipes contributed by musical Friends of the Bath
Festival but which swiftly transmogrified itself into an
anthology of the favourite romantic meals, wine and
accompanying music of the famous musicians and
singers who performed at the Festival. Some of the
recipes seem designed to encourage the reverse of
romantic fervour (Tito Gobbi's cold tinned chicken soup
mixed with milk and curry powder followed by chicken
in salt and a baked apple would severely test the staying
power of even the most smitten beau, and it is almost
impossible to imagine the romantic occasion that would
encompass chicken joints and music played by Pygmies
from the Congo – between courses only – as suggested
by Priaulx Rainier). But you could certainly warm to Peter

Maxwell Davies, whose idea of a good time involves two and a half pounds of potatoes, a pound of onions and five different wines (including a Gewürztraminer and a 1955 Condrieu). After that you'd be in no state to object to the foxtrots being played on a horn gramophone in the distance (from another room, as Maxwell Davies helpfully explains).

Many of these meals sound rather too stressful to be successfully romantic but Donald Swann solved the dilemma by bypassing the notion of dinner completely and going straight for breakfast: porridge, tea, with a copy of the *Scotsman* and a stirring rendition of Sydney Carter's *Songs of Faith and Doubt*. It might not do it for you, but the summer pudding devised by John Pritchard, Director of the Glyndebourne Festival, almost certainly would. He uses only two fruits – redcurrants and rasp-berries, which I like, but if you want a more versatile pudding, go for Jane Grigson's version in *English Food*. Whether or not to include strawberries, which form an unattractive mush when cooked? Alan Davidson's view is that 'a very few strawberries may be included. In autumn, blackberries can be substituted'. He also suggests that some varieties of gooseberry are suitable – up to you, I think. Bear in mind that you need two nights and a day to make Grigson's pudding.

Summer pudding

(from *English Food* by Jane Grigson)

Serves 8–10

> 2 lb blackcurrants or raspberries, or a mixture
>   of raspberries, redcurrants and blackberries
> 6 oz caster sugar
> good-quality white bread, one day old

Put the fruit and sugar into a bowl and leave overnight.
Next day, tip the contents of the bowl into a pan, bring
to the boil and simmer gently for 2–3 minutes to cook
the fruit lightly. It should make a fair amount of juice.
Cut the bread into slices about 1/4 inch thick. Remove
the crusts. Make a circle from one slice to fit the base
of a 2 1/2-pint pudding basin or other bowl. Then cut
wedges of bread to fit round the sides. There should
be no gaps, so if the wedges don't quite fit together,
push in small bits of bread. Pour in half the fruit and
juice, put in a slice of bread, then add the rest of the
fruit and juice. Cover the top with one or two layers of
bread, trimming off the edges to make a neat finish.
Put a plate on top with a couple of tins to weight the
whole thing down and leave overnight in the fridge.

When you want to serve the pudding, run a thin knife round between the pudding and the basin, put a serving dish upside down on top and turn the whole thing over quickly. Remove the basin and serve it with a great deal of cream. If the juice hasn't thoroughly impregnated the bread, boil up a few more blackcurrants or raspberries and strain the liquor over the white bits.

Poached pears

The smell of pears poaching with cinnamon, red wine, sugar and lemon is one of life's wintry treats; a survival from Tudor times, it fills the house with delicious Christmassy smells. There are quantities of recipes to choose from, though over the years, I've whittled it down to a combination of two of the most successful versions: Sophie Grigson's rather austere recipe (from one of her recipe cards), using water, together with Shona Crawford Poole's 'drunken pears', in *The New Times Cook Book,* incorporating a litre of red wine.

Poached pears

Serves 4

4–6 hard medium-sized pears
juice of ½ lemon
several strips of lemon zest
1 vanilla pod, split lengthways
2 sticks of cinnamon
a few cloves, and a star anise,
    if you happen to have it
110–175 g (4–6 oz) caster sugar
1 bottle of red wine

Peel the pears, leaving on the stems and preserving the shape of the fruit as much as possible, turning them in the lemon juice as you go to prevent them browning. Put the wine in a saucepan with the sugar, cinnamon, cloves, vanilla pod, star of anise and lemon zest and stir over a medium heat until the sugar is dissolved. Add the pears, bring to the boil, reduce the heat and leave to poach gently until they are tender and almost translucent (this can take anything from 1 to 4 hours, depending on size and hardness of the pears). Carefully lift out the pears and lay them in a serving dish. Boil down the remaining liquid in the pan until it is reduced to a syrupy consistency and pour over the pears. Leave to cool, and serve with quantities of thick cream, crème fraîche or mascarpone.

Gooseberry fool

'For pudding there was goosebery fool which Polly didn't like but didn't dare say so. Lydia had no such compunction. "It smells of sick," she said, "greeny, hurried sick." Nan picked her off her chair and carried her out of the room. "Strewth!" said Louise, who was given to what she thought of as Shakespearean oaths. "Poor old Lydia. She'll be for it now." And indeed they could hear muffled wails from above' – Elizabeth Jane Howard, *The Light Years*

Something of an acquired taste, a gooseberry fool,
Elisabeth Ayrton's strict encomium on the subject –
'A fool is simply a fruit cream, which should contain
nothing but fruit purée, sugar and thick cream.
Unfortunately, economical Victorian housewives saved
cream by making it up with cornflour custard which
made it almost inedible' – being indisputable. Perhaps
Lydia and Polly had got the custard kind. Having
acquired the taste, however, you should use
gooseberries. They make the best fool of all, although
you can construct satisfactory substitutes with uncooked
strawberries, raspberries and redcurrants.

Elizabeth David was adamant about how you served
a fool: 'To me it is essential to serve [it] in glasses
or simple white cups ... with shortbread or other such
biscuits.' Her recipe is the one to follow.

Gooseberry fool

(from An *Omelette and a Glass of Wine*
by Elizabeth David)

> *900 g (2 lb) green gooseberries*
> *225 g (½ lb) sugar*
> *a minimum of 280 ml (½ pint) double cream*

Wash the gooseberries (no need to top and tail them) and put them with the sugar in the top half of a double saucepan and steam them until they are quite soft. Strain off any surplus liquid and sieve them through a mouli. When the purée is cold, add the cream and more sugar if necessary. Serve à la David in individual glasses or cups.

Winter dried fruit salad

Delia has a similar one, but Pippa Small, the jewellery designer, has an incredibly easy version which looks dramatic, and the smell of the rosewater wafting from the bowl of fruits as you set it on the table is simply stunning. In my usual fashion of deciding to make something and then finding that I have only half the ingredients necessary in the cupboard, I have often improvised madly with this recipe – leaving things out and inserting rogue fruits like dried mango and guava which seems to work quite well. Go easy on the sugar, though. This is an incredibly sweet pudding and the addition of rosewater makes it swooningly aromatic. I'd serve it with huge quantities of thick cream or vanilla ice cream.

Winter dried fruit salad

(Pippa Small)

Serves 6

> zest of 1 lemon
> 200 g (7 oz) granulated sugar
> 250 g (9 oz) dried organic apricots
> 100 g (3½ oz) organic dates, stoned
> 200g (7 oz) organic figs, halved
> 200 g (7 oz) each of dried pears
>   and peaches, halved
> 100 g (3½ oz) dried organic cranberries
> 1–2 vanilla pods
> a few cardamom pods
> 2–4 tablespoons rosewater
> 1 ripe pomegranate, halved and seeds removed

Place the zest, sugar and 450 ml (16 fl oz) water in a
non-corrosive pan. Dissolve the sugar over a low heat,
then add the dried fruits, vanilla and cardamom and
simmer gently for 10 minutes. Add the rosewater, cover
and remove from the heat and leave to infuse for half
an hour or so. To serve, spoon into a dish and top the
fruits with the seeds from the pomegranate.

Apple snow

Being brought dainty little messes to eat in bed when
you're ill is, like a fading Victorian heroine, rather a thing
of the past. At least it is if you're a mother. The idea
of being an invalid, like so much else to do with the
National Health Service these days (home visits,
dentists), seems to have vanished into a black hole.
Either you are well enough to stagger out of bed and
feed the children/do the school run/go to work or you're
dead. But in 1928 you could still swing at least
a post-operative, post-childbirth month in bed to
recuperate. Or even a year, as *Everyday Meals for
Invalids* (1928) seems to indicate: its subtitle is
'a collection of tiny recipes, tasty and nourishing,
for every day of the year' and, like a stern but caring
matron, *Everyday Meals* has strict but fair rules for
convalescent care. 'Each recipe is only enough for one
person for one meal', it notes, just in case the selfish
cook was thinking of stealing a spoonful of Clothilde
Purée (six chestnuts, one small parsnip and two
tablespoons of cream, boiled, sieved and served up
with small squares of fried bread) before racing upstairs
with a tray; 'The cooking utensils must be spotlessly
clean. Dirty pots and pans are little short of criminal.
No excuse whatever can be found for a cook who puts

away a pan or basin which is not clean'; and a 'Patient's appetite must be humoured'.

This is not a book for those who espouse the 'why don't you get out of bed and move around a bit more' school of invalid care. You'd have to love someone quite a lot to go to the trouble of making a fish soufflé or braised sweetbreads for him as he languishes upstairs watching daytime TV and chatting on his mobile, and anyway, a constant supply of veal cutlets, roast pigeon and egg nog (stir one yolk, sugar, boiling milk and brandy together, then strain) might encourage the invalid to remain just that.

Everyday Meals does not run to a chapter on 'Getting them out of bed again', but if it had done, it might have have included the recipes for gruel (1 dessertspoon of oatmeal, half a pint of water or milk and a pinch of salt), linseed tea (thick) and nourishing tea (beat an egg and some milk together and slowly pour on the tea – preferably China – stirring all the time). This is a version of the method devised by Sir Kenelm Digby, whose recipes were published by his son John in 1669. 'Tea with Eggs: take two yolks of new laid eggs, and beat them very well with fine sugar. When they are well incorporated, pour your Tea upon the Eggs and Sugar, and stir them well together. So drink it hot!'. That one would be useful to know if you have a hypochondriac in the house but nothing like as useful as Mrs Rundell's Toast and Water (1806), 'good for weak bowels': 'Toast slowly a thin piece of bread till extremely brown and hard. Plunge it into a jug of cold water and leave for an hour. It should be of a fine brown colour before drinking it.'

But those of you with a real invalid to nurture could embark on the recipe for apple snow. I remember apple snow from my childhood, one of a variety of puddings designed to use up the annual apple glut from the orchard, but also perfect for invalids as it slips down easily and will contribute in a painless manner to the five fruits a day rule. This version, which is almost identical to my mother's, comes from Rose Prince's book, *New English Food*.

Apple snow

(from *New English Food* by Rose Prince)

Serves 4

> 2 egg whites
> 120 g (4 oz) golden caster sugar
> 375 ml (12 fl oz) unsweetened
>   apple sauce, puréed
> 1 pinch cinnamon
> 4 teaspoons golden muscovado sugar

Whisk the egg whites until stiff and fold in the sugar, whisk again until shiny and smooth. Mix the apple with the cinnamon and then fold into the egg white mixture. Divide the mixture among 4 glasses and sprinkle muscovado sugar on top.

Bibliography

Historical sources

Apicius, *The Roman Cookory Book* (translated by Barbara
Flower and Elizabeth Rosenbaum, Harrap 1958)

Beeton, Mrs Isabella, *The Book of Household
Management* (Ward Lock & Co. 1963; abridged version
OUP 2000)

Daudet, Marthe Pampille, *Pampille's Table* (published in
France 1919; Faber 1996)

Digby, Sir Kenelm, *The Closet of the Eminently Learned
Sir Kenelm Digby, Kt, Opened* (1669; reprinted by
Philip Lee Warner 1910)

Everyday Meals for Invalids (Stanley Paul and Co. 1928)

Farley, John, *The London Art of Cookery* (1783)

Fettiplace, Elinore, *Receipt Book* (1604, edited
and published by Hilary Spurling 1986)

Fisher, M. F. K., *How to Cook A Wolf* (Duell, Sloane
and Pearce 1942)

Four Hundred Prize Recipes (Daily Telegraph 1932)

Gerard, John, *The Herball, or General History of Plants* (1597)

Glasse, Hannah, T*he Art of Cookery Made Plain
and Easy* (1747)

The Grete Herbal (1526)

Kitchiner, Dr William, *The Cook's Oracle* (1817; Houlston and Sons 1880)

Mcilvaine, Charles, *One Thousand American Fungi* (1902)

May, Robert, *The Accomplisht Cook* (1660; five further editions, including printed for Obadiah Blagrave at the Bear and Star in St Paul's Churchyard 1685)

Midgley, Wilson, *Cookery For Men Only* (1948)

My Favourite Recipes for Dainty Dishes (Mawson Swan & Morgan 1896)

Plat, Sir Hugh, *Delightes for Ladies, to Adorne Their Persons, Tables, Closets, and Distillatories With, Bewties, Banquets, Perfumes, and Waters* (Peter Short 1600)

Mrs Rundell, *A New System of Domestic Cookery* (John Murray 1833)

Mrs Somerville, *Cookery and Domestic Economy* (Glasgow 1862)

Spry, Constance, *Constance Spry Cookery Book* (Grub Street 2004)

The Whole Duty of a Woman (1737)

Modern-day sources (post 1945)

Allen, Myrtle, *The Ballymaloe Cookbook* (Eyre Methuen 1981)

The Artist's Cookbook (introduction by Henry Moore, Macdonald Orbis 1987)

Ayrton, Elisabeth, *The Cookery of England* (Purnell 1975)

Blakeston, Oswell, *Cooking With Nuts* (Robin Clark 1979)

Bocuse, Paul, *The Cuisine of Paul Bocuse* (Granada 1982)

Buzzi, Aldo, *The Perfect Egg and Other Secrets* (Bloomsbury 2004)

Byfield, Barbara Ninde, *The Eating-in-Bed Cookbook* (Longmans 1962)

Child, Julia, *Julia Child's Kitchen* (Random House 1984)

Conte, Anna del, *Concise Gastronomy of Italy* (Pavilion 2004)

The Cookbook of the United Nations (edited by Barbara Kraus, United Nations Association 1964)

David, Elizabeth, *Mediterranean Food* (1950; compendium edition – together with French Country Cooking and Summer Cooking – Grub Street 1999)

David, Elizabeth, *French Country Cooking* (Penguin 1970)

David, Elizabeth, *French Provincial Cooking* (Penguin 1970)

David, Elizabeth, *Spices, Salt and Aromatics in the English Kitchen* (Penguin 1970)

David, Elizabeth, *An Omelette and a Glass of Wine* (Penguin 1990)

David, Elizabeth, *Elizabeth David's Christmas* (edited by Jill Norman, Michael Joseph/Penguin 2003)

Davidson, Alan, *Penguin Companion to Food* (Penguin 2002)

Ellis, Alice Thomas, *Fish, Flesh and Good Red Herring* (Virago 2004)

Fearnley-Whittingstall, Hugh, *The River Cottage Meat Book* (Hodder 2004)

The Food of Love (edited by Adrian Ball, Pitman
Publishing 1971)

Green, Henrietta, *Farmers' Market Cookbook*
(Kyle Cathie 2001)

Grey, Zane, *Zane Grey Cookbook* (Prentice Hall 1976)

Grigson, Jane, *English Food* (Macmillan 1974;
Penguin 1986)

Grigson, Sophie, *Meat Course* (Network Books 1995)

Grigson, Sophie, *Country Kitchen* (Headline 2003)

Harris, Valentina, *Risotto Risotto* (Cassell 1998)

Haycraft, Anna, and Blackwood, Caroline, *Darling, You
Shouldn't Have Gone to So Much Trouble* (Cape 1980)

Hazan, Marcella, *Marcella's Italian Kitchen*
(Macmillan 1986)

Henderson, Fergus, *Nose to Tail Eating* (1999;
Bloomsbury 2004)

Hill, Shaun, *How to Cook Better* (Mitchell Beazley 2004)

Hix, Mark, *Fish* (Quadrille 2004)

Innes, Jocasta, *The Pauper's Cookbook* (1971;
Frances Lincoln 2003)

Leigh, Rowley, *No Place Like Home* (Fourth Estate 2000)

Leith, Prue, and Waldegrave, Caroline, *Leith's Cookery
Bible* (Bloomsbury 1991)

Little, Alastair, *Keep it Simple* (Conran Octopus 1993)

MacDonald, Claire, *Delicious Fish* (Grafton Books 1986)

McEwan, Ian, *Saturday* (Cape 2004)

Norrington-Davies, Tom, *Just Like Mother Used to Make*
(Cassell 2003)

Panjabi, Camellia, *50 Great Indian Curries*
(Kyle Cathie 1994)

Pomiane, Edouard de, *Cooking in Ten Minutes* (1948;
Faber 1967)

Poole, Shona Crawford, *The New Times Cook Book*
(Collins Willow 1983)

Prince, Rose, *New English Food* (Fourth Estate 2005)

Search, Gay, and Smith, Delia, *Delia's Kitchen Garden*
(BBC 2004)

Slater, Nigel, *Real Fast Food* (Penguin 1993)

Slater, Nigel, *Real Cooking* (Michael Joseph 1997)

Spaull, Susan, and Bruce-Gardyne, Lucinda, *Leiths
Techniques Bible* (Bloomsbury 2003)

Toklas, Alice B., *The Alice B. Toklas Cookbook* (Serif 1994)

Tovey, John, *A Feast of Vegetables* (Century 1985)

Vooren, Monique van, *The Happy Cooker* (Drake
Publishers, New York, 1978)

Walsh, John, *Falling Angels* (Harper Collins 1999)

Zen, Ziggy, *How to Drink Wine out of Fish Heads while
Cooking Lobster in a Volkswagen Hub Cap* (Pan
Macmillan, Australia, 1998; Lagoon Books 2000)

Index of recipes

General index